Trails of Halifax Regional Municipality, 2nd edition

Also by Michael Haynes

Hiking Trails of Ottawa, the National Capital Region, and Beyond
Hiking Trails of Nova Scotia
Hiking Trails of Cape Breton

MICHAEL HAYNES

Trails of
HALIFAX REGIONAL MUNICIPALITY
2nd edition

GOOSE LANE

Edited by Charles Stuart.
Main cover image courtesy of Destination Halifax/ P. Jackson.
Small images by Michael Haynes, with the exception of Point Pleasant Park bandstand (Destination Halifax/P. Jackson); young girl (istock.com); butterfly (Linda and Peter Payzant); coastal village (stock.xchng); hiker's legs (istock.com).
Maps prepared by Digital Projections.
Cover design by Jaye Haworth and Julie Scriver.
Page design by Julie Scriver.
Printed in Canada on recycled paper.
10 9 8 7 6 5 4 3 2 1

Library and Archives Canada Cataloguing in Publication

Haynes, Michael, 1955-
    Trails of Halifax Regional Municipality / Michael Haynes.
— 2nd ed.

Includes index.
ISBN 978-0-86492-614-2

1. Hiking — Nova Scotia — Halifax (Regional Municipality)
    — Guidebooks.
2. Trails — Nova Scotia — Halifax (Regional Municipality)
    — Guidebooks.
3. Halifax (N.S.: Regional Municipality) — Guidebooks. I. Title.

GV199.44.C22H34 2010   796.51'09716225
C2009-907519-9

Goose Lane Editions acknowledges the financial support of the Canada Council for the Arts, the Government of Canada through the Book Publishing Industry Development Program (BPIDP), and the New Brunswick Department of Wellness, Culture, and Sport for its publishing activities.

Goose Lane Editions
Suite 330, 500 Beaverbrook Court
Fredericton, New Brunswick
CANADA E3B 5X4
www.gooselane.com

Contents

7   Introduction

15   Trails at a Glance

18   Overview Map

25   Halifax–Dartmouth

67   Eastern Shore

107   Central–South Shore

155   Acknowledgements

157   Updates from the First Edition

158   Web Pages

161   Index

Introduction

When I wrote my first book in 1994, *Hiking Trails of Nova Scotia, 7th Edition*, there were perhaps only 500 kilometres of managed footpaths in the entire province of Nova Scotia, in all its parks — national, provincial, and municipal. What has happened over the last 15 years is a truly remarkable explosion of interest in and development of paths for walking and cycling that has resulted in a system that now easily exceeds 2,000 kilometres province-wide.

Nowhere in Nova Scotia has the change been more dramatic than within the boundaries of the Halifax Regional Municipality (HRM). A wide and diversified assortment of routes has sprung into existence, largely because of the initiative of dedicated community volunteers and a small group of supportive provincial and municipal officials and politicians.

In fact, it is within the HRM that the dominant trail developments in Nova Scotia of the past decade — the conversion of abandoned rail lines to shared-use trails and the creation of back-country footpaths in Wilderness Protected Areas — has been most successful. Substantial sections of the Trans Canada Trail, built on abandoned rail lines, have opened within the HRM both north and south of its urban core. The Whites Lake and Waverley–Salmon River Long Lake Wilderness Protected Areas both boast extensive hiking trail networks, and the Bluff Wilderness Trail, though located only on non-protected crown land, is one of the finest back-country hiking opportunities in Nova Scotia.

Most residents of the Halifax Regional Municipality believe they must travel to relatively remote destinations such as the Cape Breton Highlands, Kejimkujik National Park, or Cape Chignecto Provincial Park in order to enjoy a high-quality outdoors experience. *Trails of Halifax Regional Municipality, 2nd Edition*, will introduce residents and visitors alike to many outstanding recreational pathways available close to the capital of the province.

The routes profiled in *Trails of Halifax Regional Municipality, 2nd*

Edition, are all relatively short and are generally accessible to persons of almost any physical ability. These are designed to be completed by the average walker in three hours or less and are perfect for novice hikers and visitors. Yet nothing, except possibly length, has been sacrificed in order to assemble this collection of hikes. I believe that even the most experienced outdoorsperson will enjoy many of the routes I have selected.

WHO SHOULD USE THIS BOOK

Trails of Halifax Regional Municipality, 2nd Edition, is designed to be helpful to residents and tourists alike. Every walk profiled is no more than 10 kilometres (6.25 miles) return, and no route should require more than four hours to complete. All are suitable for a summer evening stroll or a free morning or afternoon in a busy schedule.

Persons visiting the metropolitan area for only a few days who want a short, enjoyable hike will find several possibilities and a wide variety within a short distance of the downtown. If you are new to the outdoors and want to start hiking, you will find these walks are good places to begin, being reasonable lengths and, in most cases, close to residences. Families with small children who want to go somewhere for

an outdoor stroll will find most of these trails are comfortable for tiny trekkers. People with limited mobility can use almost every one of them without difficulty.

I hope you enjoy *Trails of Halifax Regional Municipality, 2nd Edition*, whatever your reason for using it, and you find that the information in it helps you, your family, and your friends to better enjoy the wonderful outdoors experiences available in Nova Scotia.

HOW TO USE THIS BOOK

I have selected 30 locations throughout the Halifax Regional Municipality where people may walk on recreational pathways that are described as trails. The walk descriptions are grouped into three regional categories to provide readers with a quick understanding of where the route is located. Eastern Shore includes trails found east of Dartmouth and, with the exception of Abraham Lake, near the coastline. Halifax–Dartmouth includes trails inside the urban core. Central-South Shore includes the areas north, west, and south of Halifax–Dartmouth.

Trails at a Glance

This index of the walks profiled in the book contains a great deal of helpful information. The Trails at a Glance may be found on pages 15-16, and should be the first place you look to decide on your next walking destination.

Length: the return distance of each route in kilometres and miles.

Degree of Difficulty: expressed as a number from 1 to 3, with "1" being suitable for almost all fitness levels, "2" exceeding 5 km (3 mi) in distance or featuring more challenging terrain and "3" exceeding 5 km (3 mi) and featuring challenging terrain, or any distance but requiring good navigation skills.

Time to Complete: approximate time required to walk the profiled route, based upon a speed of 4 km (2.5 mi) per hour, with allowances made for challenging terrain.

Permitted Uses: uses permitted on the profiled route during months when there is no snow cover:

W = walking/hiking
B = bicycling, either touring or mountain biking
I = in-line skating/skateboarding
A = ATV and other off-highway vehicles

Permitted Uses (winter): uses permitted on the profiled route during months when there is snow cover:

S = snowshoeing
X = cross-country/Nordic skiing
Sm = snowmobiling

Note: Any use marked with a * means that it is permitted and might be encountered along some sections of the profiled route, but not throughout the entire distance.

Wheelchair Accessibility: a rating of "Good" means that many wheelchair users can use the route described. A rating of "Mixed" means that wheelchair use will be possible for some, but not most, or that some portions of the profiled route are good while others are poor. A rating of "Poor" means that wheelchair use will be very difficult or impossible.

Dogs: Disagreements between dog owners and non-dog owners are among the greatest source of conflict on managed trails. Most of the trails profiled have strict regulations regarding dogs, particularly trails on municipal and provincial properties. Please observe the rules rigorously — and always "poop & scoop"!

N = no dogs permitted
L = dogs permitted on leash
O = dogs permitted off leash

Individual Route Description
Every trail is described using the same basic format. At the beginning

of each trail description is the following capsule summary:

Name of Trail: top of the page — usually the name of the park where the walk is located, the actual name of the trail if it has one, sometimes my own designation based upon a dominant natural feature.

Length: return-trip distance in kilometres (and miles) rounded to the nearest half-kilometre (quarter mile).

Hiking Time: based on an average walker's rate of 4 km (2.5 mi) per hour. Each person sets his or her own pace, which will vary according to weather conditions, the length of the trail, and individual fitness level. I suggest a time within which almost everyone should be capable of completing the walk.

Type of Trail: indicating the footing that will be encountered on the path profiled. "Crushed stone" means a surface of finely ground gravel has been spread on the route. Park trails and rail trails commonly are surfaced with crushed stone. "Compacted earth" represents the compressed surface that will be found on a dirt road or former wood road. Many provincial park trails follow former settlement roads. "Natural surface" is the unimproved

ground over which a path passes. It is common on wilderness trails and other footpaths.

Uses: possible uses are walking, biking, in-line skating, snowshoeing, cross-country skiing, and using all terrain vehicles (ATVs). The asterisk that marks some trails indicates that the use is permitted on some, but not all, of the profiled route.

Facilities: describes what services, such as washrooms, benches, garbage cans, or water, are available either at the start/finish or along the profiled route.

Rating: expressed as a number from 1 to 3, with "1" being suitable for almost all fitness levels, "2" exceeding 5 km (3 mi) in distance or featuring more challenging terrain, and "3" exceeding 5 km (3 mi) and featuring challenging terrain, or any distance but requiring good navigation skills.

Trailhead GPS: the GPS coordinates of the start/finish of the hike, expressed in latitude and longitude. This data was collected using a GARMIN GPS 12XL Receiver. It is accurate to within 25-50 m/yd.

Following the capsule summary, the main trail outline is profiled into the following sections:

Access Information: how to reach the starting point of the walk by automobile. Where possible, nearby Metro Transit stops are mentioned for those without a vehicle.

Outline: background about the trail, including historical, natural, and geographical information, as well as my personal observations or recommendations.

Brief Description: a walk-through of a profiled route, relating what I found when I last travelled this path. In every case I describe junctions and landmarks from the perspective of someone following the trail in the direction I have indicated. (If travelling in the opposite direction, remember to reverse my bearings.)

Cellphone Coverage: how well a cellphone will work on this trail, using Rogers service. Links to coverage maps of the major providers are found in the list of Web pages.

Cautionary Notes: anything that hikers on this route should particularly keep in mind. This includes: **animals:** places where bears, coyotes, and other potentially dangerous animals are more commonly found; **road crossings:** whenever a profiled route crosses a road used by automobile traffic; **hunting season:** where hunting is permitted; **cliffs**; **high waves:** during and after storms — especially during hurricane season — but any time of the year, users of coastal trails should be cautious of unexpected high waves, which can surge over trails and are extremely dangerous; **navigation:** in rare cases the profiled route may not be well signed and the ability to use a map and compass will be important; and anything that I believe you should be especially cautious about on this route will be mentioned here.

Sidebar Notes

Scattered throughout the book are brief capsule descriptions of some of the plants, animals, geological features, and human institutions that you might encounter on the various trails. These are intended to be brief samples to whet your curiosity about the world through which you are hiking, and to encourage you to learn more. Sidebar notes can be located by topic using the index beginning on page 161. Sidebar notes are indicated by a mayflower.

User Tips

Unless you are an experienced hiker, you might not know how much water to carry on your hike or why wearing blue jeans is not the best idea. An assortment of helpful hints is sprinkled among the trail descriptions. These can be located by topic using the index beginning on page 161. User tips are indicated with a hiker symbol.

Equipment

Most of the walks profiled are either very short or are surrounded by residential areas. Little special equipment is necessary. However, a few trails, notably the Admiral Lake Loop — The Bluff Wilderness Trail–Pot Lake Loop, and Crowbar Lake Trail — venture into more remote areas. For these, consider the following suggestions.

Persons travelling in Nova Scotia's woods should carry matches, a knife, and a compass — even if they have a GPS — and be able to use the compass, something surprisingly few people can actually do. Municipal recreation departments offer courses in map and compass reading, and taking one is worthwhile.

Proper footwear is essential, and there are other items that I believe you should always include as minimum equipment, even in the summer.

Water: I recommend one litre per person on a hike up to 10 km (6 mi), more if the day is hot or humid or if you are with children. Dehydration

occurs rapidly while hiking and diminishes much of the pleasure. Drink small sips of water often; do not wait until you feel thirsty to begin. I recommend you invest in a portable water filter that you always carry in your backpack

Food: Though not essential on a short hike, I always carry something to snack on. Apples, trail mix, and bagels are good, while chocolate bars, chips, and other junk food are not the best choice for several reasons. However, better something than nothing.

Whistle: If you get lost, a whistle is less likely to wear out from continuous use and will be heard far better than your voice. Always carry one.

Map: Most of the trails profiled in this book do not require a map to safely walk. However, I almost always carry a National Topographic System of Canada 1:50 000 scale map when I hike. This helps me know where nearby communities and services may be found if I do get misdirected and provides context to the walking experience. (It is rather nice to know the name of the lake you are viewing.)

Warm Sweater and/or Rain Jacket: No matter how good the forecast, always carry some protective clothing, particularly in spring and fall, or whenever you walk along the coastline.

Backpack: Invest in a day pack with adjustable shoulder straps, waist strap, large inner pouch, and roomy outer pockets. The other items I have listed will fit easily inside a good quality pack and will sit comfortably on your back. After a few trips, wearing it will become just another part of your walking routine.

Garbage Bag: Carry your trash out with you. If you carried a pop can in when it was full, carrying it out should be much easier when it is empty. Leave nothing behind except your footprints.

Optional (but recommended): Sunscreen, hat, bug repellent, camera, binoculars, field guides, first-aid kit, toilet paper, writing paper, and pen.

Hazards

There are few dangerous plants and animals in Nova Scotia and fewer still in the heavily populated Halifax Regional Municipality, especially near the metropolitan areas of Halifax, Dartmouth, Bedford, and Lower Sackville. However, it is possible to come across any of the following "critters" when you are hiking.

Bears: Black bears can be found in the more remote corners of the Halifax Regional Municipality, although they are rarely sighted. Parks Canada has an excellent brochure that I recommend obtaining. If you do sight a bear, remember that it is a wild animal capable of causing injury and even death.

Cougars: These large cats are rumoured, but not believed, to be present in Nova Scotia; none have yet been photographed, trapped, or shot.

Moose: The largest land mammals in Nova Scotia, moose are uncommon residents in the Halifax area. Dawn and dusk are the times they are most likely to be seen. Bulls can be unpredictable, especially during the fall rutting season. Moose are not just larger deer; treat one with as much respect and caution as you would a bear.

Poison Ivy: Relatively uncommon but increasing with the warming climate, poison ivy may be encountered on coastal dunes and in a few other places. An oil produced by the plant causes intense itching. (I know from personal experience.) If you think you may have found some, see a doctor as soon as possible and do not scratch or rub the affected area.

Snakes: None of the four species of snake indigenous to Nova Scotia are poisonous, but you will often find them basking in the sun beside the path, particularly in the spring and fall.

Ticks: The American dog tick is gradually working its way north through Nova Scotia and has been reported in the southern sections of the Halifax Regional Municipality. Ticks are active from as early as April to as late as July. The Nova Scotia population carries no known dangerous diseases.

Hunting Season: Usually starting in early October, hunting season varies from year to year for different types of game. Contact the Department of Natural Resources for detailed information before going into the woods in the fall. No hunting is allowed on Sundays, but always wear a bright orange garment for safety.

Weather: High winds along the coast are common, and wind chill can become significant, even in late spring and early fall. For example, you might start hiking inland at a temperature of +16°C (61°F). Reaching the coast, winds gust to 60 kph (37 mph). The wind chill equivalent becomes +6°C (43°F). Combined with water chill from ocean spray, fog, or rain, hypothermia becomes probable.

Nine Mile River

TRAILS AT A GLANCE

TRAILS OF HALIFAX REGIONAL MUNICIPALITY, 2nd Edition							
Uses (no snow): W = Walk, B = Bike, A = ATV, I = In-line Skating Uses (snow): S = Snowshoe/Walk, X = Cross-Country Ski, Sm = Snowmobile * = Permitted on some sections of the route, but not all							
Trail Name	Length km (mi)	Difficulty Level (1-3)	Time to Complete	Permitted Uses	Permitted Uses (winter)	Wheelchair Accessibility	Dogs
HALIFAX – DARTMOUTH							
Cole Harbour Heritage Park	8 (5)	2	2-3	W, B*	S, X	Good	L
Dartmouth Multi-use Trail: Sullivans Pond Lake Micmac	6 (3.75) 7 (4.4)	2 2	2 2	W, B, I* W, B*	S, X S, X	Good Good	L L
Hemlock Ravine Park	4 (2.5)	1	1	W, B	S, X	Mixed	L/O
Long Lake Provincial Park	3 (2)	3	1	W, B*	S	Poor	L
Mainland North Linear Parkway	7.5 (4.7)	2	2-3	W, B	S, X	Good	L
Point Pleasant Park	4 (2.5)	1	1	W, B*	S, X	Good	N/O/L
Shubie Park – Canal	3 (2)	1	1	W, B	S, X	Good	L/O
Sir Sandford Fleming Park	4.5 (2.75)	2	1-2	W	S, X	Mixed	L
Vivien's Way	8.5 (5.3)	2	3	W, B	S, X	Good	L
York Redoubt National Historic Site	5 (3)	2	1-2	W, B	S	Poor	L
EASTERN SHORE							
Abraham Lake Nature Reserve	4.5 (2.75)	1	1-2	W	S	Poor	O
Admiral Lake Loop	10 (6.25)	3	3-4	W, B*	S, X*	Poor	L
Clam Harbour Beach Provincial Park	4 (2.5)	1	1-2	W	S	Poor	L

Trail Name	Length km (mi)	Difficulty Level (1-3)	Time to Complete	Permitted Uses	Permitted Uses (winter)	Wheelchair Accessibility	Dogs
Crowbar Lake Trail	9.5 (6)	3	3-4	W	S	Poor	0
Gibraltar Rock Loop	2.5 (1.6)	3	2	W, B*	S, X*	Poor	L
Lawrencetown Beach Provincial Park	6 (3.75)	2	2	W, B*	S, X	Mixed	L
Martinique Beach Provincial Park	9 (5.5)	2	2-3	W	S	Poor	L
Salt Marsh Trail	8 (5)	2	2	W, B	S, X	Good	L
Shearwater Flyer: East Section West Section	10 (6.25) 7 (4.4)	2 2	3 2	W, B, A W, B, A	S, X S, X	Good Good	L L
Taylor Head Provincial Park: Beach Walk Bobs Bluff/Bull Beach Headland Spry Bay	2 (1.25) 9.5 (6) 7 (4.4) 3.5 (2.25)	1 3 3 2	1 3-4 2-3 1	W W W W	S, X S, X S, X S, X	Poor Poor Poor Poor	L L L L
CENTRAL – SOUTH SHORE							
Bedford Sackville Connector Greenway	5 (3)	1	1+	W, B	S, X	Good	L
Charles L. MacDonald Sportspark	6 (3.75)	2	2	W, B	S, X	Mixed	N
Crystal Crescent Beach Provincial Park	4 (2.5)	2	1	W	S	Poor	L
Dollar Lake Provincial Park	8 (5)	2	2-3	W, B	S, X	Mixed	L
First and Second Lake Trails First Lake Second Lake	3.8 (2.4) 2.8 (1.75)	1 1	1 1	W, B W, B	S, X S, X	Good Good	L L
Laurie and Oakfield Provincial Parks Laurie Park Oakfield Park	3 (2) 5 (3)	1 1	1 1+	W, B*, I* W	S, X S, X	Mixed Poor	L L
McCurdy Woodlot	3 (2)	1	1	W	S, X	Poor	L
Old Annapolis Valley Road	5 (3)	2	2	W	S	Poor	0
Polly Cove	3 (2)	2	1	W	S, X	Poor	0
The Bluff Wilderness Trail – Pot Lake Loop	10 (6.25)	3	3-4	W, B*, A*	S, X*, Sm*	Poor	L

Shubie Park–Canal,
Halifax–Dartmouth

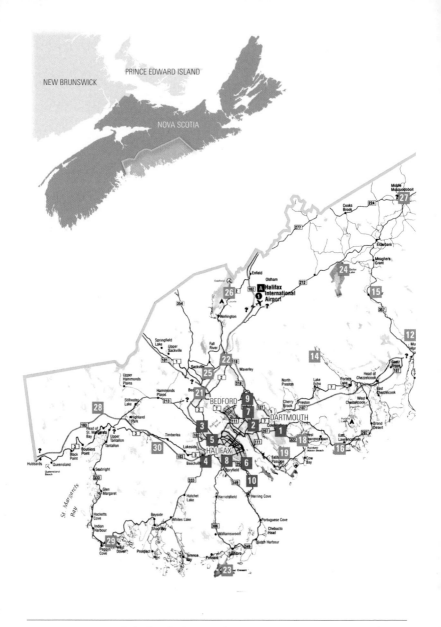

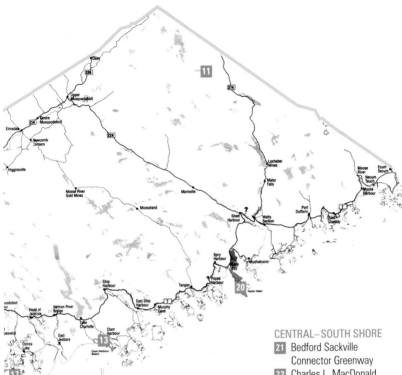

HALIFAX–DARTMOUTH

1. Cole Harbour Heritage Park
2. Dartmouth Multi-use Trail
3. Hemlock Ravine Park
4. Long Lake Provincial Park
5. Mainland North Linear Parkway
6. Point Pleasant Park
7. Shubie Park–Canal
8. Sir Sandford Fleming Park
9. Vivien's Way
10. York Redoubt National Historic Site

EASTERN SHORE

11. Abraham Lake Nature Reserve
12. Admiral Lake Loop
13. Clam Harbour Beach Provincial Park
14. Crowbar Lake
15. Gibraltar Rock Loop
16. Lawrencetown Beach Provincial Park
17. Martinique Beach Provincial Park
18. Salt Marsh Trail
19. Shearwater Flyer
20. Taylor Head Provincial Park

CENTRAL–SOUTH SHORE

21. Bedford Sackville Connector Greenway
22. Charles L. MacDonald Sports Park
23. Crystal Crescent Beach Provincial Park
24. Dollar Lake Provincial Park
25. First and Second Lake Trails
26. Laurie and Oakfield Provincial Parks
27. McCurdy Woodlot
28. Old Annapolis Road
29. Polly Cove
30. The Bluff Wilderness Trail–Pot Lake Loop

The Prince's Park

Hemlock Ravine has been a preserve of play almost since the founding of the city of Halifax. When Prince Edward, the Duke of Kent, arrived in 1794 to command the British forces in Halifax, Lieutenant-Governor Wentworth loaned him his estate on the shores of the Bedford Basin. Edward and his French mistress, Julie St. Laurent, lived here for six years at "Prince's Lodge."

Once there were man-made waterfalls, landscaped gardens, summer houses, and paths leading into the surrounding forest. Prince's Lodge was the social centre of the colony, the site of summer picnics and concerts and winter sleigh rides from Halifax to skating parties on heart-shaped Julie's Pond. Today, all that remains of this brief era of lords and ladies is the music rotunda on the shores of Bedford Basin and the names of the trails in the park.

Hemlock Ravine Park,
Halifax–Dartmouth

Village of Herring Cove, York Redoubt National Historic Site,
Halifax–Dartmouth,

Vivien's Way, Halifax–Dartmouth

Abraham Lake Nature Reserve, Eastern Shore

Jack Pine

Jack pine is the rarest of three native pines found in Nova Scotia. Its seeds require high temperatures to germinate, 44°C (111°F), so forest fires can produce a pure forest of Jack pine. It sometimes repopulates sites cleared by cutting, and might be found mixed with black spruce and post-fire hardwoods such as aspen and white birch.

Scattered pure stands are often found on sandy, barren, or poorly drained ground, something that convinced early settlers that Jack pine poisoned the soil. They also thought that its gnarled appearance meant that it was a "witch tree," and that it was to be avoided.

Look at the top of the drumlin for small to medium-sized softwoods with needles arranged in pairs. The bark is reddish-brown or dark grey and the cones are curved.

HALIFAX – DARTMOUTH

Panorama Trail, Cole Harbour Heritage Park

Tidal Marshes

Nova Scotia's tidal marshes, part of a band of salt marshes extending from the Gulf of Mexico to southern Labrador, are rich in organic materials and nutrients and are important migratory waterfowl feeding and breeding areas.

The rich ecosystem of the Cole Harbour Salt Marsh, flooded twice daily by seawater, is home to small fish, birds such as the great blue heron, and a variety of small mammals. The extensive mud flats exposed at low tide are popular with clam diggers, and hunters frequent the area during the fall migration.

A dyke similar to those on the Bay of Fundy was constructed to convert the Cole Harbour marshes to cropland in the 1800s, but was abandoned when the area re-flooded.

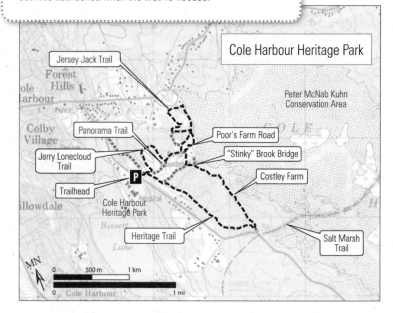

Cole Harbour Heritage Park

Length: 8 km (5 mi) return
Hiking Time: 2-3 hrs
Type of Trail: crushed stone, compacted earth, natural surface, wood chips
Uses: walking, biking*, snowshoeing, cross-country skiing
Facilities: benches, covered picnic tables, garbage cans, interpretive panels
Rating (1-3): 2
Trailhead GPS: N 44° 39' 50.6" W 63° 28' 04.3"

Access Information: From the intersection of Highways 207 and 111 near Penhorn Mall, follow 207 east for 5 km (3 mi). From Highway 207 (at this point also called Cole Harbour Road), turn right onto Bissett Road. Drive 1.5 km (1 mi); on your left is a large red barn. A parking lot is located immediately beside it.

Outline: Once the site of the Poor's Farm for the "harmless insane," this 160 ha (400 ac) property, dotted with gentle hills and bordering on the Cole Harbour Salt Marsh, is now a provincial park, and boasts an impressive and well-maintained new trail network thanks to the efforts of the not-for-profit Cole Harbour Parks and Trails Association.

The association has done an excellent job. The park's main trails are wide and covered in crushed stone, easily walkable by anyone and suitable for wheelchair use. There are benches everywhere. Paths labelled "Front Country" either retain a natural surface or have been improved by a covering of wood chips. Both surfaces offer enjoyable walking experiences, and there are many superb views of the Cole Harbour Salt Marsh both from the hilltops and at water level. For those wishing a longer walk, there is a pathway connection to both the Salt Marsh and the Shearwater Flyer trails. Biking is only permitted on the Heritage Trail.

The many interconnecting trails can cause confusion, and it is easy to find yourself heading down the wrong path. Although all major junctions are signed, the only posted maps are at trailheads.

Brief Description: From the parking area, walk to the trailhead pavilion, which features both a map and interpretive information. Continue straight on the Panorama Trail, crossing a small creek and climbing a drumlin, a large hill of fertile soil, to a junction at 150 m/yd. Turn left onto the Jerry Lonecloud Trail, which circles the cleared hillside before reconnecting with the Panorama Trail 750 m/yd later.

Turn left into the forest. Less than 200 m/yd later you emerge onto a field and have the first good views of the water, which is the Peter McNab Kuhn Conservation Area, and the Salt Marsh Trail in the distance. The path drops down the hillside, crossing a little bridge and reaching another junction at 1.2 km (0.75 mi). Continue straight, passing the Poor's Farm Reservoir on your left, and following the vegetation boundary as the path gently descends to the next junction, with the Poor's Farm Road, 150 m/yd later.

Keep straight, turning left onto the Brook Trail almost immediately. This lovely path climbs through the forest while following a small brook called "The Run," which is to your right. Barely 300 m/yd later, you reach the next junction, where you turn right onto the Jersey Jack Trail. After crossing The Run, this rougher route climbs fairly steeply up 200 m/yd to the next junction. Keep left, climbing to the top of the hill, with fields on your right and a barrier of spruce to your left. You are now on the edge of the park, and you will see houses first to your left, then ahead of you. The wood-chip-covered trail continues straight for 250 m/yd, then turns right at the next junction to drop down the water's edge, 300 m/yd further. Turn right, and follow this attractive route, boasting some of the best views of the park, 350 m/yd to the junction with the Brook and Panorama trails.

Back on crushed stone turn left, then left again when you reach the Poor's Farm Road. This trail works its way along the lower edge of a field and skirts thickets of brush. At the next junction keep left, crossing a small bridge and heading back into forest 150 m/yd later.

You reach the junction with the Costley Farm Trail, having walked 3.3 km (2.1 mi) in total. Those wishing a shorter walk should continue straight, then right when they reach the Heritage Trail. I recommend you turn left. Just 200 m/yd along you cross Stinky Brook, where the trail becomes rougher. A short side trail branching left leads to the brook's mouth, while the main trail heads into an area devastated by Hurricane Juan. For the first time, rocks jut into the treadway, which narrows

Bissett Road Farm

The Bissett Road property is crown land that was originally purchased in 1886 by the County of Halifax to create a "Poor's" Farm." Local politicians hoped that making the paupers and "harmless insane" self-sufficient farmers would be a cheaper alternative to paying their lodging at asylums in the City of Halifax.

Several expansions eventually increased the property to its present size of 186 ha (460 ac). The profile of its residents changed over the years as well, from 1901 when 35 were classified as "sane" and 23 as "harmless insane," to 1928 when 49 were classified "normal" and 87 classified "defective".

On February 28, 1929, a major portion of the institution, which by this time had grown to include several dormitories, a building for those with contagious diseases, a reservoir, and a powerhouse, was destroyed by fire. The inmates were temporarily moved to the City Home, but "The Farm" never reopened.

considerably. After 500 m/yd of this shattered landscape, the trail returns to healthier forest. At 4.1 km (2.6 mi), you reach the site of the farm, now simply an old field. Continuing along an additional 500 m/yd, now on the farm's former road, brings you to the junction with the Heritage Trail.

For those interested, the trailhead for the Salt Marsh Trail is just 50 m/yd ahead. To return to our trailhead, however, turn right, and follow the broad, bikeable Heritage Trail as it meanders back through the forest. After 250 m/yd, you pass another parking lot, on your left, but from then you proceed uninterrupted for 1.25 km (0.8 mi), mostly through storm-damaged woodlands, to the next junction. You should notice some houses, occasionally, to your left, and you pass along the edge of a field shortly before re-crossing Stinky Brook and reaching an intersection with the Poor's Farm Road. Keep straight; only 300 m/yd of attractive forest remain until you reach the trailhead and complete your walk.

Cellphone Coverage: Good throughout.

Cautionary Notes: None.

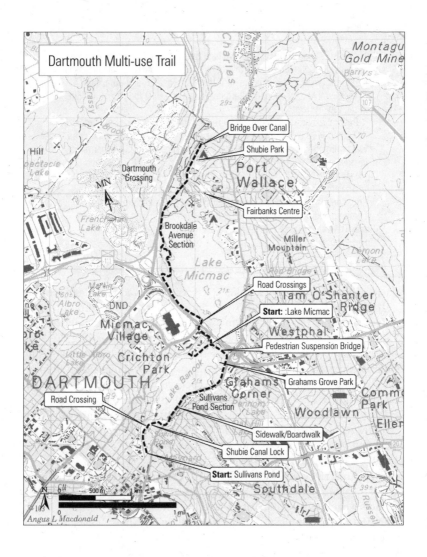

Dartmouth Multi-use Trail

Bridge Over Canal

Shubie Park

Fairbanks Centre

Road Crossings

Start: :Lake Micmac

Pedestrian Suspension Bridge

Grahams Grove Park

Road Crossing

Sidewalk/Boardwalk

Shubie Canal Lock

Start: Sullivans Pond

500 m

1 mi

Dartmouth Multi-use Trail

Length: Sullivans Pond – 6 km
(3.75 mi) return
Lake Micmac – 7 km (4.4 mi)
return

Hiking Time: 2 hrs for each section

Type of Trail: asphalt, boardwalk,
crushed stone, sidewalks

Uses: walking, biking*, in-line
skating*, snowshoeing, cross-
country skiing

Facilities: benches, garbage cans,
interpretive panels, picnic tables

Rating (1-3): 2

Trailhead GPS: Sullivans Pond –
N 44° 41' 24.1" W 63° 08' 37.8"
Lake Micmac – N 44° 41'24.1"
W 63° 08' 37.8"

Access Information: The Sullivans
Pond section starts near the junc-
tion of Ochterloney Street and
Prince Albert Road in downtown
Dartmouth, at the south end of
Sullivans Pond by the Veterans
Memorial. A burgundy sign with
white lettering marks the trailhead.
Metro Transit routes 54 and 62 have
stops alongside Sullivans Pond.

The Lake Micmac section begins
at the end of Brookdale Court. Take
Exit 4, Micmac Boulevard, from
Highway 111. Turn left at the first
set of traffic lights onto Brookdale
Crescent. Follow for 100 m/yd, turning left at Brookdale Court. Follow to
its end, 200 m/yd. There is a small
parking lot near the foot of the pedestrian bridge. Metro Transit routes
10, 54, 55, 56, 66, and 72 stop on
Micmac Boulevard, 300 m/yd from
the trailhead.

Outline: Although connected, I have
broken this trail into two routes so
that each may remain less than 10
km (6.25 mi) in length. This attractive pathway, following the shores of
lakes Banook and Micmac, is very
popular with Dartmouth residents.
Every day hundreds walk, bicycle,
and run along both sections of this
trail. Both are wheelchair accessible,
if you do not mind a crushed-stone
surface, and in-line skaters can use
the paved Sullivans Pond section.

Brief Description: Sullivans Pond
has for years been a favourite place
for parents to bring their children to
feed ducks, geese, and — of course

— gulls and pigeons, The asphalt path traces the northern border of the pond, exiting to cross Hawthorne Street and reach the shores of Lake Banook near the Senobe Aquatic and Banook Canoe clubs. A small bridge crosses the Shubenacadie Canal near one of its restored locks, and an easy climb up the gentle hill of Nowlan Street takes you to Prince Albert Road.

The trail is well signed and includes Trans Canada Trail markers. Turning left at Prince Albert Road, the route follows the sidewalk past the Micmac Aquatic Club. On the far side of this building, a boardwalk begins, tracing the shoreline of Lake Banook for the next 800 m/yd. Near Paddlers Cove is a wonderful gazebo with benches and interpretive panels, a good place to sit and watch the many paddlers who use the lake.

The trail becomes a sidewalk as it continues past Grahams Grove Park, where there are washroom facilities in the summer. Your path crosses the impressive suspension pedestrian bridge over Lake Banook, and, once across, it veers left along an asphalt pathway hugging the shoreline of Lake Banook. This attractive section continues another 500 m/yd, offering numerous benches to view the lake, before ending at Brookdale Crescent. Retrace your route to return to Sullivans Pond.

***

The Lake Micmac section is wide and surfaced by crushed stone throughout its entire length. Starting from the parking area at Brookdale, follow the sidewalk that parallels Highway 111. In 300 m/yd it reaches Micmac Boulevard, where you turn right and cross underneath Highway 111 on a crushed stone path. There are two crosswalks to negotiate, straight, then left to parallel Highway 111 for about 750 m/yd before you reach an intersection, where you turn right and descend into the woods to the shores of Lake Micmac. For the next 700 m/yd the path follows the shoreline and provides wonderful views of the shallow waters and small islands in this corner of the lake. You also pass by the remains of several former cottages that once nestled in these tiny coves.

At 2 km (1.25 mi), the trail returns to follow Highway 118 for 250 m/yd along the narrow sliver of land at the north end of the lake, before veering right. The path crosses Grassy Brook and enters Shubie Park. Numerous side trails branch to the right, but the multi-use trail continues straight up a hill before turning left within sight of a bridge crossing the Shubenacadie Canal at 2.7 km (1.7 mi). Continue straight, crossing the bridge, then immediately turn left. Follow this attractive path, which parallels and is perched above the Shubenacadie Canal, for 600 m/yd until it reaches another bridge.

There are several interpretive panels worth reading here, and you are in sight of Lake Charles, directly ahead. Connecting footpaths permit access to a small beach. If you cross the bridge and continue just a few metres/yards, you will reconnect with the Shubenacadie Canal pathway, where turning left will return you to Brookdale Court. If you return instead along your approach route to the first bridge, but do not immediately cross it, you can continue straight another 250 m/yd to reach the grounds of the Fairbanks Centre, where there are washrooms, a canteen in summer, and picnic tables.

Cellphone Coverage: Good throughout.

Cautionary Notes: Road crossings.

Hemlock Ravine Park

Length: 4 km (2.5 mi) return
Walking Time: 1 hr
Type of Trail: crushed stone
Uses: walking, biking, snow-
shoeing, cross-country skiing
Facilities: benches, dog waste
bags, garbage cans, interpretive
panels, picnic tables
Rating (1-3): 1
Trailhead GPS: N 44° 41' 18.8"
W 63° 39' 48.6"

Access Information: Lower entrance:
From the intersection of Kempt Road
and Joseph Howe Drive at Fairview
Cove, drive about 4.5 km (2.75
mi) along the Bedford Highway to
Kent Avenue. Turn left and follow
the narrow paved street uphill to a
small parking lot on the left near the
end of the road. A large signboard
displays the path network.

Upper entrance: From Highway
102, follow Kearney Lake Road
southeast toward Bedford Basin and
Halifax. After less than 500 m/yd,
turn left (at the Esso station) onto
Castlehill Drive then left again onto
Downing Street. Park on the road
next to Grosvenor/Wentworth Park

School. The trail begins at the end
of Downing Street.

Bus routes 80, 81, and 82 stop
on the Bedford Highway at Kent
Avenue, 400 m/yd from the lower
entrance. Routes 16, 33, and 86 stop
on Kearney Lake Road at Castlehill
Drive, 500 m/yd from the upper
entrance.

Outline: Hemlock Ravine is con-
sidered by many to be one of the
finest parks in the city. Located
near the former northern boundary
of Halifax, these 81 ha (200 ac) of
wooded preserve are tucked amid
one of the most rapidly developing
portions of the Halifax Regional
Municipality. The trail system is not
long; however, the network has been
developed as a maze, with numerous loops interconnecting, providing
for a considerable variety of routes.
The paths are broad and surfaced
with finely crushed gravel.

It is quite easy to become disorien-
ted in this tangle of criss-crossing
pathways, but the trails are all
named with signs posted at intersec-
tions. The trees in Hemlock Ravine

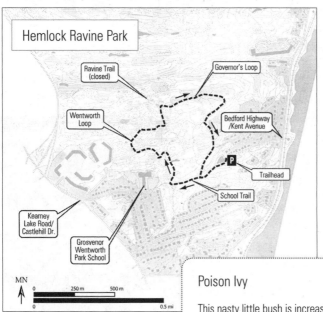

Hemlock Ravine Park

Ravine Trail (closed)

Governor's Loop

Wentworth Loop

Bedford Highway /Kent Avenue

Trailhead

School Trail

Kearney Lake Road/ Castlehill Dr.

Grosvenor Wentworth Park School

MN

0   250 m   500 m

0   0.5 mi

Poison Ivy

This nasty little bush is increasingly found throughout Nova Scotia, and if you brush against it, you might end up in the emergency room. Despite its typical three-leafed appearance, poison ivy can be difficult to recognize, as it can creep along the ground, grow as a bush, or even climb like a vine. Usually found near the edges of fields and forests, if you come into contact, you have less than 30 minutes in which to thoroughly (and I do mean *thoroughly*) wash the affected skin with cold water.

Eastern Hemlock

Dominating the slopes in the park, particularly those facing the ravine, are 300-year-old eastern hemlocks. Hemlock looks very similar to spruce but can be distinguished by its needles, which are shiny dark green above, with two narrow whitish bands on the underside. Hemlock thrives in acid soils, and often resides in pure stands in moist cool valleys and ravines, favouring north-facing slopes. The best examples of the tree in the park, towering more than 20 m (60-70 ft), are on the north-facing slope of the large ravine that makes up the park's northern boundary.

Hemlock needles are a preferred food of the white-tailed deer, and early morning visitors to the park often sight deer sharing the trails and browsing on the vegetation.

suffered less than those in Point Pleasant Park during Hurricane Juan in 2003, but the damage is enough to still be easily visible. The path descending into the actual ravine was still blocked with fallen trees in 2009.

At present, some the north slope of Hemlock Ravine remains covered by trees, and more experienced walkers will enjoy exploring its unpathed ridges. However, recent housing construction has cleared many hectares/acres of mature hemlocks and reduced the forested land accessible from the park to a small fraction of what it was less than a decade earlier. Little now remains of

the isolated and charming forest on the north slope of Hemlock Ravine.

Dogs must be leashed on all trails. The only exception is the Governor's Loop from 0900 to 1100 and from 1700 to 2000.

Brief Description: From the Kent Avenue parking lot, the broad gravelled path passes through a fence to Julie's Pond, a small, shallow, heart-shaped pool with a stone and concrete border. You can walk completely around Julie's Pond, with its flotilla of black and mallard ducks. The pond lies at the base of some quite steep hills, and there are benches for those who wish to sit and enjoy the tranquil surroundings. At dawn, you might find deer drinking from the still waters.

The School Trail leads uphill in a fairly straight line along the original route of Kent Street to connect with Downing Street near Grosvenor/Wentworth Park School, about 500 m/yd away, at the upper entrance. Several paths to the left connect the park to nearby housing. One of these short trails makes an interesting diversion; the St. Laurent Trail, nearest the school, passes a tiny stream and generally stays under attractive softwood canopy.

Turn right onto the Rockingham Loop, which leads onto rocky ridges carved by the glaciers. From the Rockingham Loop — it actually isn't a loop because it connects at both ends to the School Trail — all the other paths separate to trace their own special route through the forested terrain. After 250 m/yd on the Rockingham Loop, turn left onto the Wentworth Loop, then right at the next intersection, which occurs almost immediately. (I told you it is a maze!) The rugged terrain of the ravine forces the trail to continuously climb and descend and to constantly work its way around large rocks.

The Wentworth Loop ends on, and in the middle of, the Governor's Loop. Turn left, and 150 m/yd later, you reach the junction with the Ravine Trail, the only path that descends into the ravine itself. It narrows to single-person width and has been officially closed, blocked by fallen trees. It is along this path that the oldest hemlocks can be found, covering the north-facing slope of the park.

Your route continues along the Governor's Loop to its intersection with the Rockingham Loop in an area turned into a clearing by Hurricane Juan. Turn left and follow the Rockingham Loop back to the School Trail.

Cellphone Coverage: Good throughout.

Cautionary Notes: None.

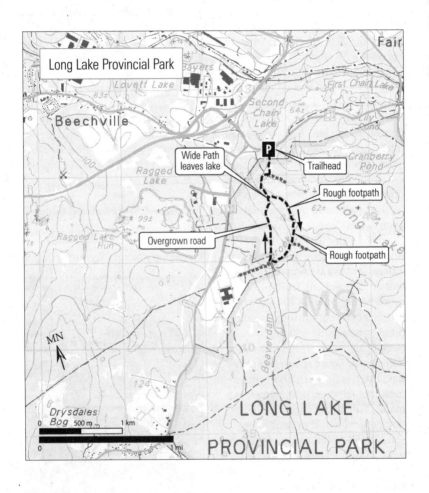

Long Lake Provincial Park

Fair

Lovett Lake

Bayers

First Chain Lake

Second Chain Lake

64±

Beechville

P

Trailhead

Wide Path leaves lake

Rough footpath

Ragged Lake

Cranberry Pond

Long Lake

62±

Overgrown road

Ragged Lake Run

Rough footpath

1±

MN

Beaverdam

MO

124

LONG LAKE

Drysdales Bog

0   500 m   1 km

0   1 mi

PROVINCIAL PARK

Long Lake Provincial Park

Length: 3 km (2 mi) return
Hiking Time: 1 hr
Type of Trail: compacted earth, natural surface
Uses: walking, mountain biking*, snowshoeing
Facilities: garbage cans
Rating (1-3): 3 [navigation]
Trailhead GPS: N 44° 37' 55.8" W 63° 39' 29.3"

Access Information: From the Armdale Rotary, follow St. Margaret's Bay Road, Highway 3, for approximately 3 km (2 mi), almost to the junction with Highway 333. On the left, you'll find a small parking area beside the road. Trailhead is signed.

Outline: Well known to local residents and dog walkers, Long Lake Provincial Park, bounded on three sides by major paved roads, can be reached by car from downtown Halifax in minutes. The park is sandwiched between Highway 306, Old Sambro Road, and Highway 333, St. Margaret's Bay Road. Some of its property crosses St. Margaret's Bay Road and borders the Chain Lakes. At its far end, it includes most of the land around Spruce Hill Lake near Harrietsfield and some of Peters Lake near Goodwood. At this point, it also connects to the northern boundary of the Terence Bay Candidate Protected Area. At its near end, it abuts North West Arm Drive and includes all the wooded land you can see between that road and Long Lake.

Every path in Long Lake Provincial Park has been created informally or is the remains of former cart tracks and Water Commission service roads. Extensive development plans have been drafted by the Department of Natural Resources, and there is some hope that formal trail construction could begin as early as 2010.

Brief Description: There are a variety of walking and biking opportunities, depending on where you enter the property. Between Long Lake and the North West Arm Drive, there are two small bodies of water, Witherod Lake and Cranberry Pond. There is an extensive network of footpaths created by several generations of residents of the area. There is also a fairly highly developed network of mountain bike trails throughout this section. These can be accessed from several spots on North West Arm Drive, and there is a broad footpath opposite the traffic lights at the Cowie Hill Connector which leads to wonderful swimming sites.

Near the junction of Dentith Road and Old Sambro Road, a variety of footpaths trace the shoreline in either direction from the dam located at the southeast end of Long Lake.

Further along Highway 306, just past the junction with Rockingstone Road, the Old St. Margaret's Bay Coach Road cuts through park reserve land to emerge on Highway 333 in Goodwood, not too far past the Exhibition Ground. Hikers and bikers frequently follow this former cart track.

Perhaps the most popular entry site, at least with dog walkers, is found on St. Margaret's Bay Road as described in the "Access Information" above. Work done when this was watershed land for the City of Halifax has cleared several pathways from the road down to the northwest end of Long Lake. From here, the challenging mountain bike trails around Cranberry Pond can be

The mouth of Beaverdam Brook, Long Lake Provincial Park

Atlantic Interior

The lands around Long Lake belong to the Atlantic Interior Region, one of eight geophysical classification zones in Nova Scotia that are defined according to distinctive landscape characteristics.

Underlain with erosion-resistant granite and quartzite bedrock, the soil is thin and has been scoured by glacial action. Chains of lakes, streams, and stillwaters have been created by poor drainage. Softwoods dominate with pockets of hardwoods found on higher, better-drained sites. The forest is interspersed with barrens and exposed bedrock, while large glacially deposited rocks, called erratics, are common.

Unlike the Atlantic Coastline, the other geophysical region making up much of Halifax Regional Municipality, wind exposure in the Atlantic Interior is a much less important factor, and summers are slightly warmer and the winters cooler.

accessed, and a former service road in the opposite direction can be followed for a short distance until you reach an earthen barricade. Expect to find dozens of walkers here on the weekends.

Once you reach the end of the broad track, turn left and follow one of the many well-worn tracks near the edge of the lake. Although sometimes challenging because of the many trees knocked over by numerous storms, you should be able to wend your way for about 750 m/yd until you reach the mouth of lively Beaverdam Brook. A distinct, but rocky, footpath parallels the creek inland, and you can follow this until it intersects the nearly overgrown remains of a former road. Turn right; this returns through the thick vegetation to the earthen barrier, about

1 km (0.6 mi) away. Expect the old road, which is usually lower than the surrounding land, to be wet and muddy, especially after any rainfall.

Those feeling energetic or somewhat more adventurous can attempt to cross Beaverdam Brook — there is no bridge, and it flows quite swiftly after any storm — and follow the indistinct and unsigned footpaths all the way to Spryfield, more than 4 km (2.5 mi) distant. Only those with excellent navigation skills should consider attempting this route.

Cellphone Coverage: Good throughout.

Cautionary Notes: Animals. No trail signage.

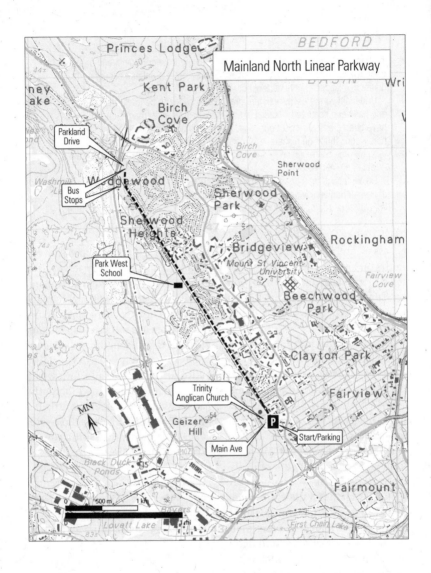

Mainland North Linear Parkway

Parkland Drive

Bus Stops

Park West School

Trinity Anglican Church

Main Ave

Start/Parking

MN

Mainland North Linear Parkway

Length: 7.5 km (4.7 mi) return
Hiking Time: 2-3 hrs
Type of Trail: crushed stone
Uses: walking, biking, snow-
  shoeing, cross-country skiing
Facilities: benches, garbage cans
Rating (1-3): 2
Trailhead GPS: N 44° 41' 24.1"
  W 63° 08' 37.8"

Access Information: From Exit 1D
of Highway 102, follow Northwest
Arm Drive to the first traffic lights,
the intersection with Main Avenue.
Turn left and continue past Veronica
Drive, about 200 m/yd. The trail en-
trance is on the right next to Trinity
Anglican Church, 321 Main Avenue.
Park on the road.

Bus routes 2, 31, and 33 stop at
the corner of Dunbrack Street/North
West Arm Drive and Main Avenue.

Route 16 stops on Parkland Drive
near the north end of the trail.

Outline: Following a major power
line for most of its length, the
Mainland North Linear Parkway is
a major active transportation and
recreational resource in the rapidly

changing district of Halifax between
Dunbrack Street/Northwest Arm
Drive and Highway 102. Used informally for years, the path beneath
the power lines was substantially
improved by the municipality with

a treadway of crushed stone, signed road crossings, and other supporting facilities.

Expect to see people at any time of the day, every season of the year. The Parkway is extremely popular with runners and bikers, who seem to enjoy its arrow-straight route and long viewplanes. With the new housing constructed on both sides of the route, more and more residents utilize every section of the trail — walking their dogs, heading to and from school, or connecting to the large shopping areas nearby.

The Heart and Stroke Foundation adopted this path as a Heart Health Trail, and it has placed kilometre and half-kilometre signage.

Brief Description: The connection of the trail with Main Avenue is somewhat obscured by recent construction; expect it to improve in future years. Currently, the path appears to be a gravel road running behind Trinity Anglican Church. However, once you reach the back of the building, you will find the trail's crushed-stone treadway heading north underneath a power line. To the left, the blinking lights on the 210 m (700 ft) communication tower at the top of Geizer Hill dominate the skyline, while on the right a number of apartment buildings border the parkway. A sign states that motorized vehicles are prohibited. In the first few hundred metres/yards, you will find several benches and garbage cans, and you can glimpse a large water tower through the trees on the left.

Westridge Drive cuts across the trail 500 m/yd from the start, permitting access to Halifax West High School and the playing fields of Mainland North Common to your left. Approximately 1.4 km (0.8 mi) from the start, four-lane Lacewood Drive is an extremely busy thoroughfare, and the greatest caution should be taken when crossing. Stay on the crosswalk. Between Westridge and

---

Leave No Trace

Leave No Trace is an international program designed to assist outdoor enthusiasts with ways to reduce their impact when they enjoy the outdoors. The Leave No Trace principles of outdoor ethics are:

- Plan Ahead and Prepare
- Travel and Camp on Durable Surfaces
- Dispose of Waste Properly
- Leave What You Find
- Minimize Campfire Impacts
- Respect Wildlife
- Be Considerate of Other Visitors

Lacewood, you also come upon the first hill on the path.

On the far side of Lacewood Drive, the path crests a small rise, providing a view of much of the next 2 km (1.25 mi). There are residences on both sides of the trail, with connector paths branching into the adjacent neighbourhoods. Continuing gently downhill, the trail crosses Radcliffe Drive 400 m/yd, later. Within 200 m/yd a playing field and track appear on your left; these are part of the Park West School, which sits beside the trail at Langbrae Drive, which you cross at 2.3 km (1.4 mi). Farnham Gate Road must be crossed 400 m/yd later.

Beyond Farnham Gate Road, the trail descends for 450 m/yd to its lowest elevation, 3.2 km (2 mi) from the start, into an area edged on the right by wooded Rockingham Ridge Park and on the left by new housing. Once again, numerous walkways branch into surrounding neighbourhoods. The trail next climbs a fairly steep hill, although this may be the most pleasant section of the walk. Older homes lining the right are partially hidden by vegetation and the left is still wooded even though several sports fields have been located there.

The climb is only 450 m/yd, and at the top is a bench if you need a rest. Heading downhill after that,

the trail continues straight for barely 100 m/yd before ending at the sidewalk of Parkland Drive. Retrace your route to return.

If you wish refreshment, turn right on Parkland and descend 550 m/yd to Kearney Lake Road. There are numerous businesses, including a large Petro Canada service station with a snack bar and washrooms and a Tim Horton's.

Cellphone Coverage: Good throughout.

Cautionary Notes: Road crossings.

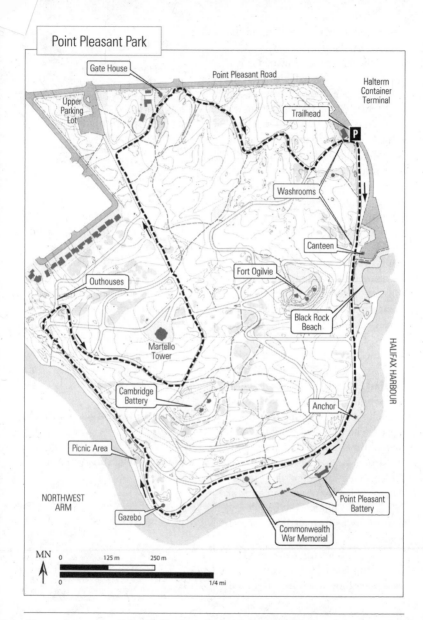

Point Pleasant Park

Gate House

Point Pleasant Road

Halterm Container Terminal

Upper Parking Lot

Trailhead

Washrooms

Canteen

Fort Ogilvie

Outhouses

Black Rock Beach

Martello Tower

HALIFAX HARBOUR

Cambridge Battery

Anchor

Picnic Area

NORTHWEST ARM

Point Pleasant Battery

Gazebo

Commonwealth War Memorial

MN

| 0 | 125 m | 250 m |

| 0 | | 1/4 mi |

Point Pleasant Park

Length: 4 km (2.5 mi) return
Hiking Time: 1 hr
Type of Trail: crushed stone
Uses: walking, biking (not
    permitted Saturdays, Sundays,
    and holidays), snowshoeing,
    cross-country skiing
Facilities: benches, canteen,
    emergency phones, garbage cans,
    gazebos, interpretive panels,
    picnic tables, unsupervised
    beach, washrooms, water
Rating (1-3): 1
Trailhead GPS: N 44° 41' 24.11"
    W 63° 08' 37.8"

Access Information: There are two principal entrances. The Upper Parking Lot is located at the junction of Tower Road and Point Pleasant Drive. The Lower Parking Lot is found where Point Pleasant Drive ends on the ocean at Black Rock Beach. Metro Transit route 9 reaches both entrances.

Outline: The best-known outdoor recreation site in Halifax, Point Pleasant Park is always full of runners, people walking their dogs, and casual strollers enjoying the matchless scenery of the entrance to Halifax Harbour. More than one million visitors stroll through it every year.

Yet few parks have suffered such a sudden, radical transformation as Point Pleasant. On the night of September 28/29, 2003, Hurricane Juan toppled 75,000 of the park's trees, more than 85 per cent of the total, including most of its magnificent mature pines. Closed for nine months for cleanup, the park's ravaged landscape and devastated shoreline shocked and saddened the entire community. An international design competition was held to plan the renewal of Halifax's iconic urban forest, and the city has responded by making significant investments in Point Pleasant's trails and other facilities.

The park's extensive network of trails permits a constantly varied route choice, and the many forts and monuments provide interesting sites to investigate and explore. The route described here roughly follows the perimeter of the park and is the most popular running route. Park

Hurricane Juan

On September 28, 2003, Hurricane Juan tracked directly up the mouth of Halifax Harbour and slammed into the Halifax Regional Municipality. Although only listed as a Category 1, the weakest possible hurricane-force storm, Juan generated destruction not seen in a generation.

Houses, boats, and electrical wires were extensively damaged, but the effect on the region's forests was particularly startling. So-called "wind-bombs," exceptionally powerful gusts generated near the storm's centre, completely flattened sections of forest through-out the HRM, including almost all the thousands of mature pines that roofed Point Pleasant Park.

The effects of Hurricane Juan were so devastating to the region that Environment Canada requested, successfully, that the World Meteorological Organization officially retire the name "Juan" from its rotating list of hurricane names. The effects of Juan can still be seen on many of the parks and trails.

Point Pleasant Park gatehouse

hours are 6:00 a.m. to midnight, but the parking lot gates are closed at 9:30 p.m., with Lower Lot B shutting at 8:00 p.m. from mid-April to mid-October.

Brief Description: Starting at Lower Lot A beside the Shakespeare-By-The-Sea office, where there are public washrooms, follow the broad Sailors Memorial Way toward Black Rock Beach. Numerous signposts greet you, and provide reams of information. You will also soon notice that every path junction sports new and easily legible directional signage.

After 200 m/yd, you reach the canteen next to Black Rock Beach at the Lower Parking Lot. Continue along Sailors Memorial Way. On the left is the entrance to Halifax Harbour; most days vessels ranging from small sailing craft to warships and transatlantic container ships will be in sight. Fort Road and Prince of Wales Drive branch to the right, while benches and picnic tables can be found every few metres/yards.

As the trail curves around the end of the peninsula, a number of monuments and ruins can be found. The large anchor is from Canada's last aircraft carrier, HMCS *Bonaventure*, and commemorates members of the armed forces who lost their lives at sea during peacetime for whom there is no known grave. The crumbling concrete ruins surrounded by a fence, Point Pleasant Battery, were part of the harbour defences during World War II.

After topping the first tiny rise, 700 m/yd from the start, you will sight the Commonwealth War Memorial, dedicated to the individuals of the navy, army, and merchant navy of Canada who lost their lives at sea during World War I and II. This large memorial is lit at night so that it may be visible to the crews of incoming ships.

Sailors' Memorial Way traces the coastline, climbing a small hill crowned with a gazebo before turning right to follow the deep indentation of the Northwest Arm. Your route is now known as Arm Road, which passes the site of the former Purcell's Cove Ferry, recently extensively developed as a picnic area. The path here climbs gently for a further 500 m/yd.

You next encounter a small clearing and a major trail junction, as well as a large map of the park. Continue on Cable Road, turning right onto Serpentine Road just before the impressive new stone washrooms. Now you are climbing more steeply as your route turns through more than 180° as it moves up the hill and away from the ocean. Continue straight at the next junction, Tower Hill Road, and the second, about 200 m/yd further, where you will be on Maple Road. At the next major junction, Cambridge Drive, you will be able to see the ruins of Cambridge Battery on your right. Turn left, or take a few minutes to explore the site.

You are now on one of the busiest sections of trail in the park. On the left is the Martello Tower National Historic Site, and paths lead there 200 m/yd up the trail. For nearly 500 m/yd, Cambridge Drive is straight and nearly level, coming to within 50 m/yd of the Upper Parking Lot before turning right onto Lodge Road. This short trail passes by Quarry Pond and the fascinating Gate House before reaching Point Pleasant Drive and Young Avenue at Centennial Pond.

On the far side of the fountain there, you re-enter the park on Birch Road. From here your route is almost all downhill, descending past the only sizeable marsh in the park. Several smaller trails branch off to either side, but after 500 m/yd you encounter a T-junction. Turn left, following the path back to Lower Parking Lot A.

Cellphone Coverage: Good throughout.

Cautionary Notes: High waves during and after storms.

Shubie Park – Canal

Length: 3 km (2 mi) return
Hiking Time: 1 hr
Type of Trail: crushed stone
Uses: walking, biking, snow-
shoeing, cross-country skiing
Facilities: benches, canteen,
garbage cans, interpretive
panels, washrooms, water
Rating (1-3): 1
Trailhead GPS: N 44° 42' 08.6"
W 63° 33' 15"

Access Information: From the MicMac Parclo, follow Route 318, the Waverley Road, north for 2 km (1.25 mi). Turn left onto Locks Road just past the traffic lights. Watch for a sign for the Fairbanks Centre. Follow Locks Road to a large parking area 600 m/yd from Waverley Road.

Metro Transit route 55 stops on Waverley Road.

Outline: Situated on the banks of the Shubenacadie Canal route, connecting Lake Charles and Lake Micmac, Shubie Park is a popular recreational retreat for many local residents throughout the year. Its many footpaths provide a variety of options, and the canal is popular with canoeists and kayakers.

The Fairbanks Centre is operated by the Shubenacadie Canal Commission and contains exhibits about the history of the canal. There is a self-guided interpretive walk along the route of the canal and brochures are available at the centre, which is open from May 24 until Labour Day.

Bring something to feed the ducks. The sheltered waters of the canal are home to hundreds in the late fall and winter, and in spring the flooded margins provide excellent nesting areas for ducklings. The area by the trailhead is even signed as a "Waterfowl Feeding Area."

Brief Description: From the parking area, begin your walk at the signpost near the pond. Turn right, and strike out along the broad gravelled walkway as it follows the east bank of the small pond. Like most of the paths along the canal, it is wide enough for two and composed of compacted gravel. Approximately 300 m/yd later, you encounter the first bridge

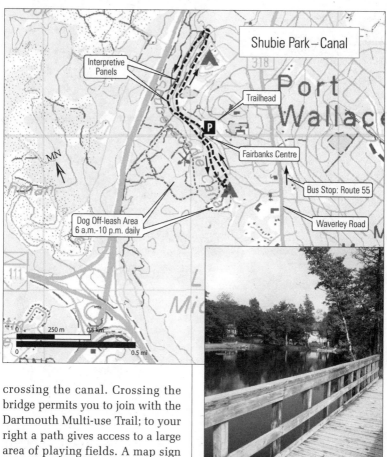

Shubie Park – Canal

Interpretive Panels

Trailhead

Port Wallac

Fairbanks Centre

Bus Stop: Route 55

Waverley Road

Dog Off-leash Area
6 a.m.-10 p.m. daily

MN

250 m   0.5 km
0.5 mi

L
Mic

crossing the canal. Crossing the bridge permits you to join with the Dartmouth Multi-use Trail; to your right a path gives access to a large area of playing fields. A map sign indicates your present location.

Continue straight. Your route climbs the small ridge above the canal and follows the water route. This section narrows at places and several rocks and tree roots extrude from the gravel, but the footing is still reasonable for all fitness levels.

The canal is to your left, at times as much as 10 m/yd below, while on your right you will be able to see playing fields and the Shubie Municipal Campground through the fringe of trees.

For a short time the path moves out of sight of the canal, the water becoming visible again about the same time you see Lake Charles directly ahead. Shortly afterward, you reach another bridge, 800 m/yd from the parking area. Beyond the bridge is a small beach with changing rooms, and to the right, washrooms are available when the Shubie campground is open.

Across the bridge, there is another map sign and a three-way junction. To the right, a short path leads to the shore of Lake Charles; straight ahead a connector permits access to the Dartmouth Multi-use Trail. Turn left and take the route bordering the

Spare Socks

After walking for a couple of hours, changing into a fresh pair of socks is almost as refreshing as bathing your feet in cool water, and you will find a new spring in your step. I carry two extra pair so I have one to change into at the end of the hike.

canal. This section offers the best treadway of the system, wide and bordered by wooden beams to contain the gravel. Frequent interpretive panels profile the building of the Shubenacadie Canal. The path stays very close to the waterway, following the crest of the narrow cut until returning to the first bridge, 1.4 km (0.8 mi) into your walk.

The trail descends to water level as it returns to the pond near the Fairbanks Centre. On your right, you will notice that much of the woodland has been flooded so that the trail is a causeway for almost 200 m/yd. At the end of the pond, you may cross a bridge and return to the parking area. Otherwise walk straight, passing alongside Lock 3. Notice the small dock on the lower side of the lock, permitting canoeists to portage around the structure.

At 2 km (1.25 mi), the trail reaches a dirt road. Lock 2 is just beyond it, and this is the end of the improved trail. Both a dirt path and a gravel road continue the remaining 200 m/yd to the shore of Lake MicMac near the entrance to the canal. From here you can see the MicMac Parclo, Micmac Mall, and the small islands dotting the lake. To your right is an off-leash area for dogs.

Below Lock 2, a small footbridge conducts you back to the east bank. Turn left after crossing the bridge and, when you reach the road, look for the crushed-stone pathway about 10 m/yd to the right. The trail now passes between the canal and nearby houses with a fence separating it from backyards. For the final 350 m/yd the trail follows the waterway until it reaches the grounds of the Fairbanks Centre and the parking area.

Cellphone Coverage: Good throughout.

Cautionary Notes: None.

Coyote

Nova Scotia's most recently arrived large mammal resident is also one of its most elusive. Clever, adaptable, and unbelievably resilient, coyotes arrived in Nova Scotia as a continuation of their eastward migration across the continent. The first coyote kill was in 1977, and today coyotes are widespread throughout the province.

Eating almost anything, including plants and berries, coyotes prefer snowshoe hare and other small mammals, even cats from homes near Long Lake.

Rarely exceeding 30 kg (65 lb), coyotes resemble large brownish-grey dogs. Accustomed to being shot on sight by farmers and hunters, coyotes are quite shy about allowing themselves to be seen. Usually all you will find is scat in the middle of the trail, with the fur of recent kills mixed through it.

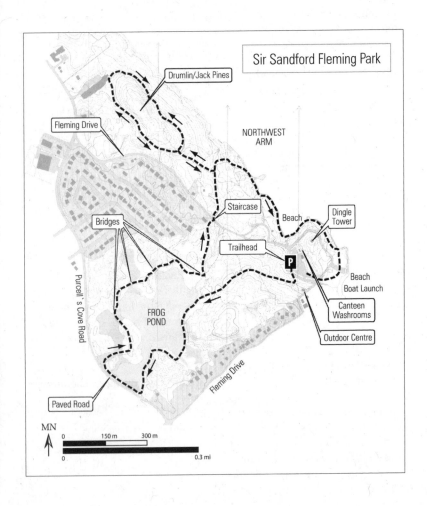

Sir Sandford Fleming Park

Drumlin/Jack Pines

Fleming Drive

NORTHWEST ARM

Staircase

Beach

Dingle Tower

Bridges

Trailhead

Beach Boat Launch

Canteen Washrooms

Outdoor Centre

Purcell`s Cove Road

FROG POND

Fleming Drive

Paved Road

MN

0   150 m   300 m

0   0.3 mi

Sir Sandford Fleming Park

Length: 4.5 km (2.75 mi) return

Hiking Time: 1-2 hrs

Type of Trail: crushed stone, dirt tracks

Uses: walking, snowshoeing, cross-country skiing

Facilities: benches, canteen, emergency phones, garbage cans, picnic tables, playground, unsupervised beach, washrooms, water

Rating (1-3): 2

Trailhead GPS: N 44° 37' 45.1" W 63° 35' 52.2"

Access Information: From the Armdale Rotary, drive up Herring Cove Road, turning onto Purcell's Cove Road at the first set of traffic lights. Continue approximately 2 km (1.25 mi) to Fleming Drive and turn left. Watch for the park entrance sign. Immediately past the stone gates, take the first left, Dingle Road, and follow it to the parking area by the canteen.

Metro Transit route 15 runs along Purcell's Cove Road, and there are stops near both the park entrance and the Frog Pond parking area.

Outline: A beloved family recreation site near peninsular Halifax, yet still seemingly remote, Fleming Park offers a variety of activities throughout the year. The beaches are popular sunning locations, and the adjacent boat ramp is busy throughout the summer. The Frog Pond is a favourite duck feeding location, and in winter, this small pool is popular with skaters.

Sir Sandford Fleming Park is L-shaped, with one arm dominated by a large hill and the other by Frog Pond. The principal paths circle each of these commanding features, and the Dingle Tower and the lower parking lot are situated at the base. The route I describe starts from the lower parking area and explores both arms, ending on the beaches. Either loop can be walked separately for a shorter, 2 km (1.25 mi) walk.

Brief Description: From the interpretive map panel in the parking area, take the trail to the left of the maintenance shed up the hillside opposite the Dingle Tower. At the first trail junction turn right and follow this crushed-stone path through the woods until you reach Frog Pond, about 400 m/yd later. Turn left. For the next 500 m/yd, the trail follows the edge of the water until it reaches the pavement of the Purcell's Cove Road.

Turn right and walk alongside the road — not in the bike lane — for the next 150 m/yd until you reach the upper parking lot. This part of Frog Pond is thick with ducks waiting to be fed, and a platform with picnic tables is an excellent place to watch them. At the end of the parking lot, a broad path heads into the woods, continuing the circuit of the pond. You will cross several sizeable marshy areas with long, un-railed bridges providing dry passage. Follow this path, ignoring frequent side trails, until you cross a bridge spanning a small brook in very stony ground. Turn left and, almost immediately, turn left again across another bridge. For the next 200 m/yd, follow an old cart track through attractive spruce and hemlock before reaching a wooden staircase next to a house.

At the bottom of the steps, you may either turn right and return to the starting point or turn left, cross the road, and take the path entering the woods. Follow this downhill about 175 m/yd, past a park maintenance area, and turn left. The next 150 m/yd includes 45 m/yd of climbing, the most challenging part of the walk. You encounter a broad pathway that circles the hill 30 m/yd below the summit and may turn either left or right because this is a loop trail. If you feel energetic, try one of the paths leading to the crest. The summit is much higher than the Dingle Tower, and you will find a stand of Jack pine, one of the few growing in Halifax Regional Municipality parklands.

Descend the same path you climbed, and when you reach the junction at the bottom, turn left. Passing two small ponds, you reach the Northwest Arm within 150 m/yd. Follow the compacted gravel walkway along the ocean's edge. Your car is less than 400 m/yd away, although

Layering

Instead of having a separate outfit for each weather condition, put together a variety of clothes for different purposes: base (underwear), insulation, and outer shell. Mix and match according to conditions, adding, removing, or changing items as you warm up or cool down and if weather conditions change. Synthetic clothes for layering tend to be lighter, more durable, and provide greater flexibility.

 ### Sir Sandford Fleming

Fleming Park is named after Sir Sandford, who moved to Halifax in the 1880s when he was engineer-in-chief for construction of the Intercolonial Railway. Fleming conducted the initial survey for the Canadian Pacific Railway, designed the first Canadian postage stamp, and earned the title "Father of Standard Time" for his work on the present system of time zones.

He donated his 38 ha (95 ac) summer retreat, The Dingle, on the Northwest Arm, to the city in 1908.

The Dingle Tower was built to serve as a memorial to the development of parliamentary institutions in the British Empire. At a ceremony that drew members of the Royal Family and dignitaries from throughout the British Empire, the Governor-General, the Duke of Connaught, dedicated the 10-storey structure. The Royal Colonial Institute of London donated the bronze lions at the foot of the tower in 1913.

the path continues around Dingle Cove and traces the perimeter of the point on which the tower was constructed. This section is especially attractive at dawn and dusk, with many interesting homes and properties visible on the opposite shoreline. The Northwest Arm is usually active with sailboats and other small craft, and you pass a small beach with its boat launch and nearby playground just before you finish your walk. (Dogs are not permitted on the beach.)

Cellphone Coverage: Good throughout.

Cautionary Notes: Walking on road.

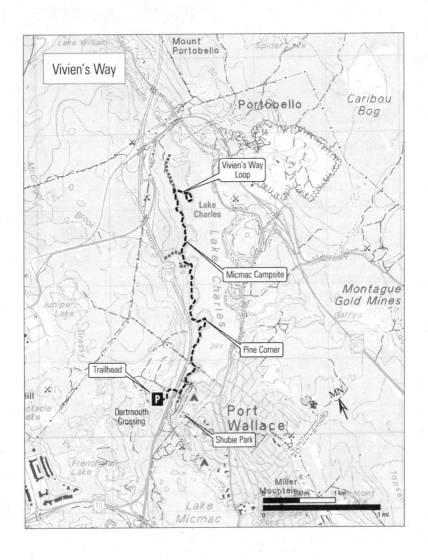

Vivien's Way

Mount Portobello

Lake William

Spider Lake

Caribou Bog

Portobello

56

Vivien's Way Loop

Lake Charles

Lake Charles

Micmac Campsite

Montague Gold Mines

Barrys

Juniper Lake

Grassy

116

28±

Pine Corner

107

70

MN

Trailhead

P

Dartmouth Crossing

Port Wallace

Shubie Park

French Lake

Miller Mountain

Lake Micmac

Topsa

500 m   1 km

0   1 mi

Vivien's Way

Length: 8.5 km (5.3 mi) return
Hiking time: 3 hr
Type of Trail: asphalt, compacted earth, crushed stone
Uses: walking, biking, snowshoeing, cross-country skiing
Facilities: benches, garbage cans, picnic tables
Rating (1-3): 2
Trailhead GPS: N 44° 42' 22.9"
W 63° 33' 33.2"

Access Information: From the MicMac Parclo, drive northwest on Highway 111. At 1.2 km (0.75 mi), take Exit 4N onto Highway 118. In 2 km (1.25 mi), exit right at NS 118. Turn left onto Wright Avenue. In 500 m/yd, turn right onto Countryview Drive. After 400 m/yd, turn left onto Shubie Drive. Continue to the end of the street, about 300 m/yd, and park in the lot beside the trail.

Metro Transit route 56 stops on Countryside Drive, 500 m/yd from trailhead.

Outline: The Shubenacadie Canal and waterway, beginning in Halifax Harbour and connected by lakes and rivers to the Bay of Fundy, was the first "superhighway" in Nova Scotia. Although work started in 1826, difficult terrain and primitive construction methods prevented its completion until 1861. By then railways were already in operation, and they drove the canal company out of business in 1871.

The Shubenacadie Canal Trail follows much of this route, connecting downtown Dartmouth to the restored locks in Shubie Park and the Portobello Inclined Plane. For much of its length, it traces the shoreline of Lake Charles. This is an excellent shared-use pathway, broad and surfaced in crushed stone, frequently providing easy access to the water, and meandering through mostly young hardwood forest. Longer walks are possible, but the route profiled here makes an excellent afternoon hike for the entire family.

Brief Description: Follow the asphalt pathway around the parking lot and over busy, multi-lane Highway 118 on a dedicated pedestrian bridge. Once across, take either the stairs or the winding bike ramp down the hillside to the crushed-stone Shubenacadie Canal Trail. In the 350 m/yd en route, you will cross a road, and pass a garbage can, a dog waste bag dispenser, and some informational signage.

Turn left, and follow the wide, well-maintained pathway as it parallels Highway 118. Almost immediately, you pass a trail junction, which would connect you to the Shubenacadie Canal. A short 100 m/yd detour to your right, will take you to a bridge over this historic waterway and to an interesting interpretive panel.

Continue straight, passing a few benches before reaching a junction at 750 m/yd. You might also notice a distance sign, facing in the return direction, which reads "Lake Charles 6.2 km to Halifax Harbour." If you go right at this junction, the path circles around the top of a hill, providing views of Lake Charles, before reconnecting with the Shubenacadie Canal Trail.

Keep left; the path drops down the hillside to the bottom of the embankment of Highway 118, then turns right to thread the narrow corridor remaining between road and lake. Now at water level, the trail follows the shoreline for a con-

siderable distance before cutting behind a thickly forested knoll. At 1.5 km (0.9 mi), the route makes an extremely sharp left turn; a sign tells you this is "Pine Corner 7.2 km."

Once again you descend to lake level, curving around a small cove. Within 300 m/yd, you reach an area of storm damage, where the trees covering a considerable area were flattened. The trail skirts the edge of this area for about 100 m/yd, passing a picnic area on your right that overlooks the lake, then curves left and works through the open area for another 250 m/yd before returning to healthy forest.

Within 250 m/yd, you cross a study bridge over tiny Cooks Brook. A side trail that branches to your left takes you 200 m/yd to the top of a knoll, where there are good lake views when the trees are without leaves. Another bridge is crossed 150 m/yd later. The side trail here is somewhat longer, climbing the hillside to your left to cross underneath Highway 118 in a massive culvert, where it ends. If you are in the mood for exploring, it might be fun to follow, but there are no views or connections elsewhere.

When you reach the sign "Micmac Campsite 8.6 km," you have travelled approximately 3 km (1.9 mi). This lovely spot, situated above the lake on your right, might be worth

Belted Kingfisher

One of the most effective of the fishing birds, the kingfisher dives headfirst into the water after any small fish that ventures too near the surface. Easily recognized by its ragged crested head and bluish-grey back, wings, and tail, belted kingfishers are so adept that it was once permissible to shoot them at any time of the year in order to protect young trout and salmon from their depredations.

You will probably hear a kingfisher before you sight it. Disturbed by your approach, it will abandon its perch on a limb or power line overhanging a lake or stream and skim the surface of the water to a safer location while loudly making its distinctive rattling call.

a visit. Little footpaths drop down to the water. For the next 300 m/yd, the trail meanders out of sight of the lake, passing through attractive woodlands. When you reach the lake again, its shores are lined with rocks and towering pines, enabling easy access should you wish to dip your toes.

Another 500 m/yd brings you to the junction with the Vivien's Way side trail. The Shubenacadie Canal Trail continues straight for another several kilometres/miles, but I suggest you turn right onto this naturally surfaced footpath. Vivien's Way circles a slender finger of land jutting into Lake Charles and hosts both benches and picnic tables. You will also find a bronze plaque that commemorates the contributions of Vivien Srivastava, for whom this delightful loop is named. This is a wonderful place to enjoy a lunch and go for a refreshing swim on a hot summer day.

Vivien's Way adds only 800 m/yd to your walk. When you return to the crushed-stone surface of the Shubenacadie Canal Trail, turn left, and retrace your route back to the trailhead.

Cellphone Coverage: Good throughout.

Cautionary Notes: Road crossing.

York Redoubt National Historic Site

Length: 5 km (3 mi) return
Hiking Time: 1-2 hrs
Type of Trail: crushed stone, dirt
    tracks
Uses: walking, biking, snowshoeing
Facilities: benches, garbage cans,
    interpretive panels, washrooms,
    water
Rating (1-3): 2
Trailhead GPS: N 44° 35' 53.7"
    W 63° 33' 11.6"

Access Information: From the Armdale Rotary, drive up Herring Cove
Road, turning onto Purcells Cove
Road at the first set of traffic lights.
Continue approximately 8 km (5 mi)
to the second entrance to Fergusons
Cove Road, and turn left onto it.
Watch for the National Historic Site
sign, but continue past the entrance
and turn at the next right by a large
church. Drive past the church and
park at the end of the road.

Metro Transit route 15 runs along
Purcell's Cove Road and stops in the
parking area of the redoubt.

Outline: During World War II, York
Redoubt was one of the most important elements in the Halifax defence
system. Today, it has become a quiet
location for a picnic or a short walk.
Every ship entering and leaving
Halifax must pass through the narrow channel between York Redoubt
and McNabs Island. From the gun
emplacements, 55 m/yd above the
waterline, this offers an unrivalled
view of all the military and civil-
ian traffic moving in and out of this
busy port.

The trails are not well known,
and most days you will encounter
few other hikers. The profiled route
takes you along the roads that connected the various bunkers, gun
emplacements, and other structures
of the complex. These structures are
in varying states of disrepair, and
caution should be exercised before
exploring any ruins. Please respect
posted warning signs.

Brief Description: Your route initially follows the old Chapel Hill
Road, which skirts the outer edge
of the fortification wall, running
level along the slope of the hillside. On your left, the ground falls

McNabs and Lawlor Islands

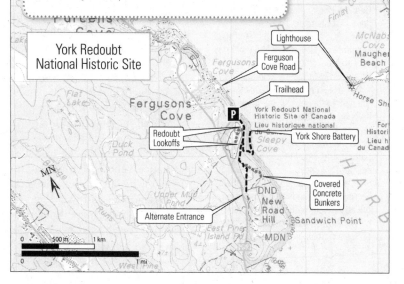

McNabs Island Lighthouse and Hangman's Beach, York Redoubt

From the battery at York Redoubt, the entrance to Halifax Harbour is nearly blocked by two large, unpopulated islands that have both played important roles in the story of Halifax. McNabs, the larger of the two and the one facing the main entrance to Halifax Harbour, was the site of several fortifications that were an important part of the port's defence system. Lawlor Island, opposite the Eastern Passage near Shearwater, was a former quarantine station and hospital site, and many victims of cholera and flu epidemics are buried here.

A community interest group, The Friends of McNabs Island Society, is spearheading efforts to see the islands advanced as a park development. They organize beach cleanups, picnics, and other activities, and have published a book, *Discover McNabs Island*, that outlines the natural and cultural history of this fascinating natural preserve.

York Redoubt
National Historic Site

Lighthouse

Ferguson Cove Road

Trailhead

York Redoubt National
Historic Site of Canada
Lieu historique national

York Shore Battery

Redoubt Lookoffs

Covered Concrete Bunkers

Alternate Entrance

DND New Road Hill

Sandwich Point

0   500 m   1 km

0   1 mi

Halifax Fortifications

Halifax was founded because of its valuable harbour, and one of the first goals of British authorities was to protect it. A system of forts, including Georges Island, the Citadel, Fort Needham, Fort Clarence, Fort Ives, and other installations, was all part of the elaborate and layered defences of this vital Imperial city. Halifax became the most heavily fortified site in Canada.

Located on a steep bluff overlooking the narrowest point in the outer harbour, York Redoubt had a useful life that extended from 1793 until the end of World War II. Initially the site of gun batteries designed to engage attacking surface vessels, the installation of a submarine net across to nearby McNabs Island and the construction of the searchlight battery and supporting guns on the shoreline made this one of Halifax's most important defensive positions.

away steeply, descending 45 m/yd in the 70 m/yd to the ocean. However, the old road is broad, level, and well surfaced, and makes for easy walking. Baby strollers can, with some difficulty, be manoeuvred over this surface.

About 150 m/yd from the start, access to the Redoubt can be gained through the sally port, which is open from 9 a.m. to 6 p.m. when the Historic Site is operating. On the left, you may notice a footpath plunging toward the ocean, but this is far rougher and narrower than the main route. Chapel Road continues straight, and after a further 150 m/yd, it reaches the junction with Sleepy Cove Road, where a bench has been placed. Turn left, following the road down the hillside for 300 m/yd. Near ocean level, the trail cuts sharply left and continues a further 300 m/yd to end at the site of the York Shore Battery. An interpretive panel profiles the history of this World War II emplacement, access to which was prohibited in 2009.

Returning along the same route, you will notice a narrow footpath entering the woods to the left at the bend in Sleepy Cove Road before it begins the steeper climb back to Chapel Hill Road. This short side trail leads to the entrance of a cave-like opening in the hillside. If you want to explore, make sure you have a flashlight and waterproof footwear.

Once back on Chapel Hill Road, turn left and follow it through some magnificent hardwoods just outside the fortification wall. Approximately 250 m/yd further, another old road branches off to the left. This dead end, perhaps 400 m/yd long, heads to the site of several concrete ruins over which wooden shelters have been constructed to protect them. Chapel Hill Road continues straight, gradually narrowing until it is little wider than a footpath. You might notice damage from a massive forest fire in the area in 2009.

The road ends at the parking lot

beside the main building of the Canadian Naval Engineering School's Damage Control School, which is on the Purcells Cove Road. To return to the start, retrace your route for 1 km (0.6 mi).

If the Redoubt is open, enter through the 50 m/yd underground sally port and explore the fortifications. This should be the highlight of your visit as this National Historic Site contains numerous interpretive panels, superb views from the Fire Command Post — the building located at the highest point of the site — and dozens of cannon, some still mounted and facing the harbour. (None still work, disappointingly.) You will also find wheelchair-

Sally port entrance

Sally port interior

accessible washroom facilities, with electricity and flush toilets, on the west side of the parking lot.

Following all the paths and exploring inside the fortifications, you can enjoy more than 5 km (3 mi) of interesting and varied walking through a significant historical site.

Cellphone Coverage: Good throughout.

Cautionary Notes: Some dangerous structures, little signage.

Fortress curtain wall at York Redoubt

EASTERN SHORE

Clam Harbour Beach Provincial Park

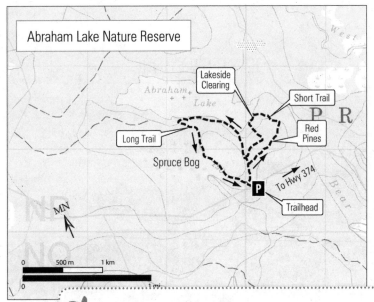

Abraham Lake Nature Reserve

Lakeside Clearing

Short Trail

Abraham Lake

Long Trail

Red Pines

Spruce Bog

To Hwy 374

MN

P

Trailhead

0   500 m   1 km

0   1 mi.

Nature Conservancy of Canada

For more than 45 years the Nature Conservancy of Canada has been acquiring and protecting natural areas. In 1994, it accepted ownership of the 343 ha (846 ac) Abraham Lake Forest Preserve from Scott Maritimes Ltd. Containing one of the few old growth stands of red spruce, eastern hemlock, and white pine remaining in Nova Scotia, this pocket of pre-European forest has survived centuries of harvesting, and extensive forest fires. For 25 years previously, Scott Maritimes has maintained this forest preserve.

The Conservancy intends to preserve the forest around Abraham Lake as a "living classroom," dedicated to conservation education. In addition to the area of "cathedral forest," so-named for the high cathedral-like canopy of the old growth trees, a 206 ha (509 ac) buffer zone has been established surrounding it.

Abraham Lake Nature Reserve

Length: 4.5 km (2.75 mi) return
Hiking Time: 1-2 hrs
Type of Trail: natural surface
Uses: walking, snowshoeing
Facilities: none
Rating (1-3): 1
Trailhead GPS: N 45° 09' 34.3"
    W 62° 36' 46.1"

Access Information: From Sheet Harbour, 111 km (69 mi) from Halifax, drive 34 km (21 mi) toward New Glasgow on Highway 374. Look for a sign on the left that reads "Governor Lake." Turn left, and drive 5 km (3 mi) on the dirt road; a large sign indicating the trailhead is on the right. There is a parking area with a large trailhead pavilion.

Outline: The trail around Abraham Lake, deep in the heart of the Liscomb Game Sanctuary, was constructed because of its stands of mature hemlock and red spruce. In 2006, the Abraham Lake Nature Reserve, owned and managed by the Nature Conservancy of Canada, was extended protection under the Special Places Protection Act.

This hike follows a well-marked path through gently rolling terrain and is suitable for families and persons of most fitness levels. However, be cautious using the trail during hunting seasons, even though hunting is not permitted on this property. Signage has improved: red-and-white metal rectangles mark the Short Trail and orange and white the Long Trail. Many other markers from earlier signage programs also remain.

Reaching Abraham Lake requires driving into an area of the province to which few people travel, the interior between New Glasgow and Sheet Harbour. Abraham Lake is quite remote, and you should let someone know when you are going in and when you are expected back.

Brief Description: The trail immediately heads into the forest under a canopy of young trees. The area bordering the road is a buffer zone to protect the older trees against the effects of natural disturbances as well as provide habitat for animals and birds. At the first junction, just

inside the woods, head right. Soon afterward, you walk beneath tall spruce. Because of the thick canopy overhead little understorey thrives. Only ferns lift above ground level, and a carpet of rich green moss dominates.

The trail is distinct and easy to follow, moving gently along a hillside to cross the tiny brook and bog draining Abraham Lake. Climbing again, you encounter another junction, this with a sign pointing right stating "Short Trail — 30 minutes." (Note: trailhead sign says it will take 45 minutes to complete the short trail.) This may be the most attractive section of the hike, cresting a tiny hill underneath the 30 m/yd high red spruce. It is very still beneath their massive interlocking boughs; wind and sunlight are virtually excluded here.

Very shortly, your path turns sharply left and reaches the shore of Abraham Lake. Loons frequently nest here, so do not be surprised if you hear their call as you approach. There is a small clearing along the lake's bank ideal for a picnic. The path continues close to the lake, turning inland once across the brook to follow it back to another junction. Signs indicate turning left to return to the start, turning right for the Long Trail — 45 minutes. (The trailhead sign says this will take 2 hours.)

The Long Trail returns to the lakeshore, following it for the next 1.5 km (1 mi). At several places, the path cuts a swath through the middle of a dense thicket of very young trees, providing a decidedly tunnel-like aspect. Turning sharply left you enter a region of old-growth hemlock. For the first 200 m/yd, the path is difficult to follow, and you must rely upon the posted signs until a spruce bog on your right and rising ground on your left provide a clearer indication of the route. The final leg heads directly toward the parking lot, passing through an area of old-growth birch and maple along the way. Shortly after crossing another tiny creek, the loop ends at the junction near the parking lot. Turn right for the last 100 m/yd.

Cellphone Coverage: None.

Cautionary Notes: Animals.

Admiral Lake Loop

Length: 10 km (6.25 mi) return
Hiking Time: 3-4 hrs
Type of Trail: compacted earth, crushed stone, natural surface, rocks
Uses: walking, biking*, snowshoeing, cross-country skiing*
Facilities: benches, garbage cans, outhouses, tables
Rating (1-3): 3
Trailhead GPS: N 44° 47' 38.3"
    W 63° 08' 59.1"

Access Information: From Dartmouth, drive east along Highway 107, then take Highway 7 to Musquodoboit Harbour, approximately 40 km (25 mi). Turn left onto Highway 357 for 200 m/yd. Turn right at the trail sign; a large parking lot is on the left approximately 50 m/yd further.

Outline: If you like rocks in large volume, particularly granite, then this is the trail for you. Although possibly the most challenging hike found in this book, the Admiral Lake Loop comes with my highest recommendation. This walk is only for the fit, but you are rewarded with magnificent views. Wear your sturdy footwear for this one and carry lots of water. Do not forget either binoculars or camera and expect sore muscles afterward.

If you wish something easier, walking along the Musquodoboit Trailway, an abandoned rail line to the end of Bayer Lake and returning along the same route permits a pleasant 5 km (3 mi) saunter with no vertical climb.

Brief Description: For the first 2.5 km (1.5 mi), follow the Musquodoboit Trailway, part of the Trans Canada Trail. You cross the Musquodoboit River on the old steel truss bridge, now decked and with railings, a few hundred metres/yards from the start. At 1 km (0.6 mi), you will find a signpost — 13.5 km is written on its opposite side — and the first of many benches.

At 1.8 km (1.1 mi), you reach the first trailhead of the Admiral Lake Loop junction to your right. A large wooden map shows both its route and that of the short Bayer Lake Loop. Tempting though it might appear, I recommend that you continue past this entry point.

For most of the next km (0.6 mi), the trail squeezes between Bayer Lake and a massive granite rock face on the right. Several benches face the lake. At 2.3 km (1.5 mi), a covered picnic table, bench, and bicycle rack sit beside a tiny sandy beach. Perhaps 100 m/yd further on the right is a new outhouse and, beyond that, another reconstructed bridge on the rail line.

However, between the outhouse and the bridge, a slender footpath leaves the rail bed and begins to climb the steep hillside. There is another map of the trail system posted here, and a Trans Canada Trail Discovery panel about the pink lady's slipper. Instead of graded, level track, this footpath is rugged, rocky, and covered in moss and lichen. Ascending the reverse slope of the hillside, the trail arrives at a splendid viewing platform, signed "Jessie's Diner," on the bare granite summit. You can see far up and down the Musquodoboit River Valley and easily spot the covered table on the rail line 45 m (150 ft) below.

Immediately the trail descends through dense conifers until it reaches a tiny brook 300 m/yd from

Jessie's Diner. Cutting sharply left you climb again, until you notice small Eunice Lake through the branches ahead to your right. Your route is never level, moving up and down the innumerable knolls and skirting the many granite boulders left behind by the glaciers. The trail finally touches the edge of the pond about 3.5 km from the start of the hike. Shortly before it does, you reach a junction with the South Granite Ridge section of the Whites Lake Wilderness Ridge Trail, which branches left, and where there is another trail system map. Don't go that way by mistake, or you are in for a very long walk indeed!

Continuing past Eunice Lake, you reach an area where the few trees are mostly young birches. The trail works around a massive bare knoll until the approach is from the less challenging northwest. At its top, the Admiral Lake Lookoff, you have another outstanding view. Inland, to the east, you can see Admiral Lake and several prominent granite knolls and cliffs, while the Atlantic Ocean is visible to the southwest.

Following the ridge to the southeast, the path works downhill for the next 300 m/yd until it crosses a small brook. Once across, the trail climbs again, moving alternately from cleared area into thick trees. About 500 m/yd beyond the brook,

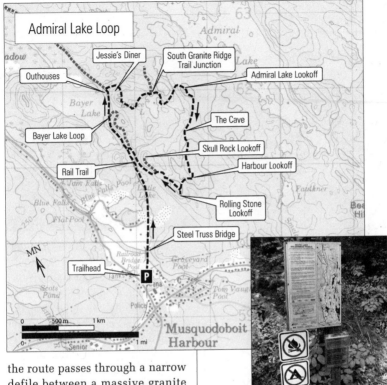

Admiral Lake Loop

Jessie's Diner

South Granite Ridge Trail Junction

Outhouses

Admiral Lake Lookoff

The Cave

Skull Rock Lookoff

Bayer Lake Loop

Harbour Lookoff

Rail Trail

Rolling Stone Lookoff

Steel Truss Bridge

Trailhead

Musquodoboit Harbour

the route passes through a narrow defile between a massive granite outcropping and a huge fragment that has broken off it. This cramped passageway, The Cave, may be too narrow for you and your pack together.

For the next 400 m/yd, the trail works through thick spruce, emerging only to trace bare granite ridges. The route is cunningly crafted to take advantage of folds in the land, rocks, and the parallel ridges, and you are delivered perfectly positioned

for a superb view of Petpeswick Inlet at the Atlantic Ocean lookoff. Immediately afterward, the trail descends steeply, and a rough stairway has been constructed to permit passage. Even so, this is the most challenging section of the hike.

At the Rolling Stone Lookoff, there is another magnificent view, a superb sight of the steel truss bridge on the abandoned rail line nearly 100 m/yd

Skull Rock Lookoff

Bald Eagle

As you approach the truss bridge crossing the Musquodoboit River, look closely at the tall spruce trees on the far bank. In the early morning, if there have not been many hikers already, you may sight a bald eagle perched and looking for prey.

These massive birds are enormously popular with visitors. In Nova Scotia, their numbers have increased rapidly in recent years and at times more than 200 have been sighted simultaneously.

With a wingspan reaching 2-2.5 m (7-8 ft), and its distinctive white head, this majestic bird is unmistakable in flight, slowly riding the air currents with as little wing movement as possible. Once killed indiscriminately as a pest, it is now illegal to kill or injure an eagle in Nova Scotia.

below. After this, the trail begins its final, rapid descent. However, to your right in about 300 m/yd is a side trail to the Skull Rock Lookoff. Although only 250 m/yd long, this side path is rugged and rough; the view is worth the effort, however. The main trail continues to descend, passing beneath Skull Rock and crossing a genuinely lovely brook and the junction with the Bayer Lake Loop in the last 500 m/yd before rejoining the abandoned rail line at the first signpost. Turn left and follow the rail trail back to the parking area.

Cellphone Coverage: Good throughout.

Cautionary Notes: Animals, cliffs, isolated area, rugged terrain.

Clam Harbour Beach Provincial Park

Length: 4 km (2.5 mi) return
Hiking Time: 1-2 hrs
Type of Trail: cobbled beach, natural surface, sandy beach
Uses: walking, snowshoeing
Facilities: canteen, changing rooms, garbage cans, outhouses, payphone, tables, water
Rating (1-3): 1
Trailhead GPS: N 44° 43' 47.8" W 62° 53' 07.3"

Access Information: From Dartmouth, drive east to the end of Highway 107, then on Highway 7 to Lake Charlotte, approximately 58 km (36 mi). Turn right onto Clam Harbour Road; watch for the blue park sign. Drive 10 km (6 mi). The park entrance is an unpaved road to the right, and the parking area is 600 m/yd further along. Park your car in the picnic area to the right of the main lot. Gates close at 9:00 p.m.

Outline: Home to the annual Beach Sand Sculpture Contest, Clam Harbour is a popular destination on hot summer weekends. With its wide, long beach and relatively easy coastal trail, Clam Harbour is an excellent location for novices to begin with a short, but very pleasant, walk. The large changing house and canteen building offers water and flush toilets and also contains a display area outlining the human and geological history of the area.

Even from October to May, when the park is closed, this is a good location for a relatively easy hike. Walking in from the gate will add only 1.2 km (0.75 mi) to the total distance.

Brief Description: The picnic grounds are located atop a drumlin overlooking the beach. Tables, benches, and outhouses are spread among the trees and fields, and you will also find the original Stoddard family burial grounds, dating from the early 1800s, surrounded by a white picket fence. A long staircase permits an easy descent to the beach, about 10 m/yd below.

Lifeguards are on duty Saturdays and Sundays during the summer, but they cover only a small part of

the beach. Signs warn swimmers to be cautious of the dangerous undertow. At the base of the stairs, a wide brook on your right limits the walk in that direction, so turn left and follow the 20 m/yd wide sandy beach for nearly 1 km (0.6 mi). The view oceanward is magnificent. Clam Bay is broad and scattered with islands, and the waves roll in ceaselessly from the southwest. To your left, you will see the park structures containing the washrooms and restaurant.

At the end of the beach, where the first rocky outcropping intrudes into the sand, a vehicle track cuts through the dune grasses and extends the hike toward Burnt Point. Just off the beach is a junction,

and there are outhouses on the left path. Continue straight, following the vehicle track past a tiny brackish pond to a turnaround area. From here, the trail narrows to a footpath paralleling the coastline just above the high-water mark. There is even the occasional hiking sign.

For the next few hundred metres/yards, the path crosses rocky headlands and small, sandy beaches. Even though the route is easy to follow, clearly worn into the vegetation, some might find the walk challenging where the brush grows quite thick. Soon, however, you emerge onto a coastal barren, the path open and unobstructed. Almost directly ahead, the lighthouse on Long Island will draw your attention.

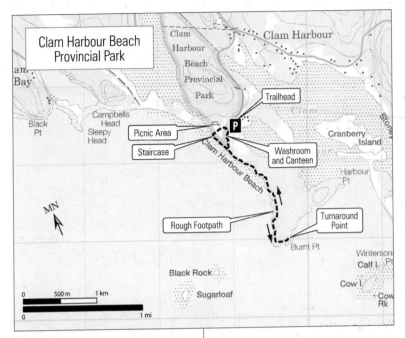

Clam Harbour Beach Provincial Park

The final 500 m/yd are on the exposed headland of Burnt Point, the path ending in a series of rocky ridges sloping into the water. A tiny headland, nearly cut off from the mainland, is the turnaround point of the hike. Narrow paths lead up to its rocky summit, from where you gain a wonderful view of Clam Harbour.

Beyond Burnt Point, the path disappears, replaced by broken rock formations that run at right angles to the coastline. I recommend that the less hardy walker proceed no further. Anyone choosing to continue will face a rugged scrabble for another 1 km (0.6 mi), until the rocks are replaced by the marshes on the inland face of Burnt Island and Harbour Point.

On your return to the park grounds, leave the beach at the lifeguard station. An extensive boardwalk and bridge system will lead you to the parking lot and the canteen building.

Cellphone Coverage: None.

Cautionary Notes: High waves during and after storms.

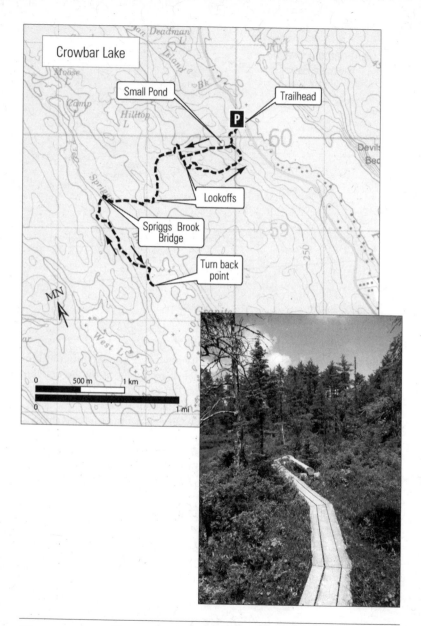

Crowbar Lake

Length: 9.5 km (6 mi) return
Hiking Time: 3-4 hrs
Type of Trail: natural surface
Uses: walking, snowshoeing
Facilities: benches
Rating (1-3): 3
Trailhead GPS: N 44° 47' 44.6"
W 63° 22' 37.8"

Access Information: From the Mic-Mac Parclo, drive east on Main Street (Highway 7) for 8.5 km (5.3 mi). This becomes Highway 107, which you follow for 11 km (6.9 mi) to Exit 19. Turn left onto West Porters Lake Road; continue 1.4 km (0.9 mi) to Highway 7. Turn left for 200 m/yd, then turn right onto Myra Road. Follow for 8.3 km (5.2 mi); the trailhead parking lot is on the left.

Outline: The Crowbar Lake Hiking Trail is located in the Waverley-Salmon River Long Lake Wilderness Area, a rugged pocket of pristine lakes, high granite ridges, and diverse vegetation, including old-growth pine and hemlock, found relatively close to the urban centre of the Halifax Regional Municipality.

The route profiled is only a fraction of the complete trail system. Anyone planning to hike this route should be aware that it will require a high level of fitness to complete and will take you into remote terrain where cellphones will not necessarily work. Adequate preparation, including packing food, water, and extra clothing, is essential. I also strongly advise notifying people where you are heading and when you expect to return.

This is a challenging trail, but it is a rewarding one that takes you through splendid wilderness terrain. Those new to hiking should not begin with this route, but after you gain more experience and comfort, it should definitely be high on your "to do" list.

Brief Description: From the parking area, a rustic sign indicates where the narrow footpath leads immediately up the hillside, curving its way around the many boulders strewn everywhere. A rough-hewn railing provides assistance, and a map of the trail system is posted at its top.

Spriggs Brook Bridge, Crowbar Lake

Tree-mounted red metal markers designate the route. Within seconds, you will realize how challenging this walk will be; the rugged, rocky landscape requires careful foot placement, and the steep hillside quickly causes your heart rate to elevate. You will also notice many fallen trees, a legacy of the damage caused by Hurricane Juan in 2003.

Various regulatory signs dot the first few hundred metres/yards. You should have plenty of time to read them as you labour uphill. But within 400 m/yd, the path levels off, and you find yourself on a boardwalk next to a tiny, tranquil pond. There is even a rough-hewn log bench. At 500 m/yd, you reach the first junction; keep right, where you begin a very challenging climb up a steep hillside to the next junction, 600 m/

yd later, where you will find another system map.

Now more or less at the top of the hillside (thankfully, in my case), after a brief additional climb, the narrow, but distinct, footpath begins to gradually descend, meandering through thick vegetation, with few views available except for one small area of bare rock, for the 1.8 km (1.1 mi) to Spriggs Brook. As you approach the stream, more and more moss covers the hillside. When the path levels off, a treadway of rocks conducts you over the boggy ground, and a first, unrailed, log bridge — very slippery when wet — traverses a small branch of the brook. When you reach the main creek, less than 50 m/yd later, a much more impressive structure, considerably elevated above water level and with railings, provides access to the other side. You will also find another trail map posted here.

Once across Spriggs Brook, the trail climbs and soon turns left to parallel the stream. Within 500 m/yd, the path drops back to water level for a short distance but then climbs again to follow a beautiful pine-covered ridge, where there are some good views of Spriggs Brook. The trail continues along this ridge for several hundred metres/yards, then turns away from the water and climbs another ridge. But this is a brief punishment because the path soon curves left around a spur and drops back to water level, coming right to the shore of Granite Lake.

By now you have walked a little more than 4 km (2.5 mi). The trail traces Granite Lake for another few hundred metres/yards, and there are several excellent locations along its pine-lined banks where you might rest and enjoy a snack. The wilderness hiking trail, however, continues for much further. Once the path turns away from the water and begins to climb the next ridge, you should turn back. If you continue, about 300 m/yd uphill, you will reach the next junction, with the West Lake Loop, completing which would add 4.5 km (2.8 mi).

Instead, enjoy a pleasant respite beside Granite Lake. When you are ready, retrace your approach route back over Spriggs Brook and to the junction at the top of the hill above the first small pond. Once here, turn right. This 800 m/yd descent provides some of the best views of the hike, including some of Porters Lake, and takes you through an area of remarkable, and oddly impressive, storm damage. (The massive felled trees bring to mind dinosaur skeletons.) This path reconnects to the main trail in the fern-covered

Wilderness Protected Areas

In 1998, Nova Scotia declared 31 parcels of crown land to be Wilderness Protected Areas. This partially met a commitment of the federal government and all provincial governments to complete Canada's network of protected areas by the year 2000. Subsequently, a number of other areas have received similar protection.

The lands selected as Wilderness Protected Areas are representative examples of Nova Scotia's typical landscapes and ecosystems, so designated in order to protect their rare or outstanding natural features or processes, and to provide recreational opportunities.

The 4,558 ha (11,262 ac) White Lake Protected Area just to the west of the Musquodoboit River offers outstanding wilderness travel opportunities because of its interconnected lakes and its extensive trail network.

ground just before the small pond. Turn right; 500 m/yd remains to the trailhead.

Cellphone Coverage: None at trailhead or in low-lying areas. Good on hilltops and at both Granite Lake and the Spriggs Brook Bridge.

Cautionary Notes: Animals, isolated area, rugged terrain.

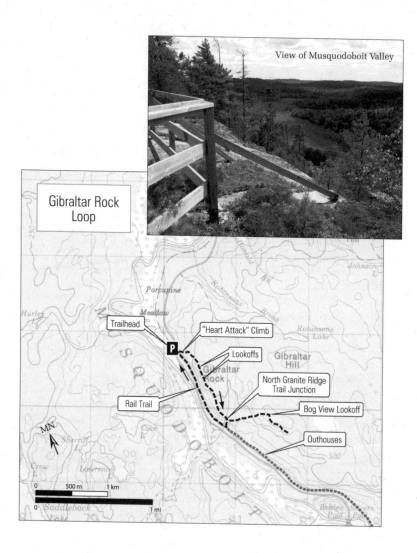

View of Musquodoboit Valley

Gibraltar Rock Loop

Trailhead

"Heart Attack" Climb

Lookoffs

Gibraltar Rock

Porcupine

Meadow

Hurley

Johnson L.

Robinsons Brook

Robinsons Lake

Gibraltar Hill

North Granite Ridge Trail Junction

Bog View Lookoff

Rail Trail

Outhouses

MN

Sherriff L.

Cove

Crow

Lowrence

Saddleback Lake

Bridge Pool

0   500 m   1 km

0   1 mi

Gibraltar Rock Loop

Length: 2.5 km (1.6 mi) return
Hiking Time: 2 hrs
Type of Trail: compacted earth, natural surface, rocks
Uses: walking, biking*, snowshoeing, cross-country skiing*
Facilities: benches, garbage cans
Rating (1-3): 3
Trailhead GPS: N 44° 53' 28.4" W 63° 15' 00.4"

Access Information: From Dartmouth, drive east along Highway 107, then Highway 7, to Musquodoboit Harbour, approximately 40 km (25 mi). Turn left onto Highway 357 and follow it for 15.5 km (9.7 mi). Turn right at the trail sign into a large parking lot.

Outline: Do not be deceived by the short distance of this walk; it is a killer! (Maybe not literally, but those with known heart issues might want to consider something less challenging.) Simply put, this trail climbs up a very steep hill to an attractive lookoff and then descends almost as steeply as it ascended.

But what a view you earn, and what a fascinating area of the province to explore. Gibraltar Rock is part of the Granite Ridge natural history region, a prominent feature along the Eastern Shore extending nearly 80 km (50 mi) in length and 8-10 km (5-6.25 mi) in width. The area is characterized by jutting, steep-sided hills that rise sharply from the ocean, with cliffs common, creating a plateau area 100 m/yd above sea level. The Whites Lake Wilderness Protected Area, which this trail borders, lies within the Granite Ridge region.

The Musquodoboit River has carved a narrow gorge through the craggy hills, making the views of it from Gibraltar Rock quite dramatic and the main reason for undertaking this challenging climb.

Brief Description: Start along the abandoned rail line, part of the Trans Canada Trail. A sign says that an outhouse is 1.7 km (1.1 mi) from the trailhead. Barely 60 m/yd past the metal gate, the Gibraltar Loop Trail, 1.3 km (0.8 mi), separates to

Abandoned Railroads

Railroads were the superhighways of the late 19th and early 20th centuries, the only practical method to move goods and people over land before the invention of the automobile. Every community vied for a railway connection: having a rail station meant prosperity and growth; being passed by meant decline and economic stagnation.

By the end of World War II, however, railroads were unmistakably in decline, and most of the province's branch lines, and even a few main routes, were abandoned. Yet their role in transportation is not over, for in the past two decades hundreds of kilometres of rail lines have been converted to recreational trails, such as the Shearwater Flyer and the Salt Marsh trails.

the left. As soon as you are off the former rail line, you begin to climb — think of a staircase but without steps.

The narrow footpath is signed with yellow metal flashes, and you will need to watch for them because the terrain is extremely rocky. As you are beneath a canopy of hemlock and spruce, it is almost impossible to distinguish the path from the rest of the hillside. Large granite rocks litter the landscape, and the path picks its way among them as best it can.

The first few hundred metres/ yards are exceptionally difficult, a punishing scramble. Fortunately, there are places where rocks have been piled and a few guardrails have been placed, so something has been done to provide assistance. There is a little levelling in 100 m/yd, and you pass in front of a rock face at 250 m/yd. Expect your calves to be burning and the sound of your pulse throbbing in your head.

Surprisingly quickly — or maybe not, depending upon your level of fitness — you emerge onto the bare expanse of Gibraltar Rock, where a fence provides both safety from the cliff and a welcome place to rest and recover. There is an attractive view of the river below and the valley it has created. Expect it to be windy and possibly hot because the few Jack pines growing here provide neither shade nor shelter.

The path continues uphill over the exposed rock, but more gently, and parallels the ridge, though it is set back somewhat. Sometimes the metal flashes are red as well as yellow. After another 150 m/yd, you reach a second lookoff, this one including a bench dedicated to the memory of Patrick Elhorn. From here the trail begins to descend, imperceptibly at first, but more noticeably as you continue.

The footpath is narrow, barely one person wide, and full of tree roots and rocks, as it wends its way down the slope. You will notice many dead trees littering the forest floor and sometimes almost acting as fencing for the path. These were all destroyed in one night in 2003 during Hurricane Juan, and at times, the surrounding woods look as if there was a massive clear-cut, but instead of the trees being removed, they were piled into gigantic heaps. For almost 400 m/yd, the trail picks its way through this surrealistic debris heap; the rebuilding of this section was a huge challenge for the trail volunteers because the original path had been completely obliterated and buried beneath hundreds of fallen trees.

Suddenly, as if passing from one room to another, you return to tranquil and picturesque forest. The contrast could not be greater. Perhaps 100 m/yd later, you cross a slender footbridge, cleverly fashioned from the trunks of two trees with railings added, and reach the junction with the Wilderness Trail. There is a map, so you can see your options, and a sign tells you that Kelly Junction, the next waypoint along the North Granite Ridge Trail, is 9 km (5.6 mi) away.

But you turn right, following the yellow flashes, and now drop precipitously down the hillside. On this section, you are assisted by several staircases, some of stones and at least one cunningly cut into a fallen log — again with a handrail. The descent is rapid, perhaps only 150 m/yd, before you cross another rough footbridge and reconnect with the abandoned rail line. At this junction, there is a trail system map, and a sign indicates that there are outhouses 600 m/yd to your left.

However, unless your need is great, your return to the trailhead is to the right, a gentle 1.1 km (0.7 mi) stroll along the broad, flat, and level Rail Trail, which parallels Highway 357.

Cellphone Coverage: None at trailhead and on lower slopes. Good on hilltop.

Cautionary Notes: Animals, cliffs, isolated area, rugged terrain.

Old Shoelaces

Sounds silly, but old shoelaces take up very little room and can be invaluable. (And if you think nothing will ever break at an inconvenient moment, good luck.) If you carry a small tarp, you can quickly erect a shelter by tying it between trees using the old laces.

Lawrencetown Beach
Provincial Park

Stoney Beach

Road Crossings

Atlantic View Trailhead Pavilion

Conrad Beach

Lloy

Fox Point

Lawrencetown Head

Lawrencetown Beach

Lawrencetown Prov Park

Trailhead

MacDonald's Tea Room

MN

Egg Island

Half Island

0   500 m   1 km

0   1 mi

Lawrencetown Beach Provincial Park

Length: 6 km (3.75 mi) return

Hiking Time: 2 hrs

Type of Trail: boardwalk, crushed stone, natural surface, rocky cobble, sandy beach

Uses: walking, biking*, snowshoeing, cross-country skiing

Facilities: benches, canteen, changing rooms, garbage cans, interpretive panels, supervised beach, washrooms, water

Rating (1-3): 2

Trailhead GPS: N 44° 38' 37.1" W 63° 20' 56.6"

Access Information: From the Mic-Mac Parclo, drive along Highway 111 toward Cole Harbour for 2 km (1.25 mi). At Exit 7E, turn onto Route 207 and drive for approximately 19 km (12 mi). Park at the first, small parking area on the right at the bottom of the hill, just before you reach the Lawrencetown Beach Provincial Park entrance.

Outline: Lawrencetown Beach has become extremely popular with surfers. Even in winter it is common to observe several of these enthusiastic individuals, covered from head to toe in their high-tech insulating suits, riding their colourful boards through the large waves common to this stretch of coastline.

The area is popular with swimmers as well, but it has a tragic reputation. Because of the combination of intense wave action and brisk outflow from Lake Echo and Lawrencetown Lake, a strong undertow is a regular feature at Lawrencetown and nearby Conrad beaches. Almost every year, a few people encounter difficulties. Swimmers should stay on the supervised section and only enter the water when lifeguards are on duty.

Until protected by legislation in the 1960s, beaches like Lawrencetown were "mined" for their sand. At the eastern end of the beach, you will find several areas where the dunes were extensively quarried.

Brief Description: From the parking area facing the ocean, head to the beach and turn left. Enjoy nearly 1.4 km (0.9 mi) of pristine sand as waves pound the exposed shore and tiny shorebirds skitter along the edge of the constantly advancing and retreating surf. When you are about 100 m/yd from the houses at the east end of the beach, turn inland, and carefully follow a clearly defined footpath until it intersects the abandoned rail line. This runs parallel to the beach and the highway and provides the best view of both the dune system and the bird and plant life.

Turn left; the rail line path heads directly toward the park's building, becoming boardwalk when you reach the parking area. There are washrooms and a canteen at the building, although both are open only in the summer. Continue past, keeping on the boardwalk, until you reach the highway, 2.8 km (1.75 mi) from the start of your walk.

Here you will find the trailhead pavilion for the Atlantic View Trail, including several interpretive panels and a map of the Cole Harbour/Lawrencetown Coastal Heritage Park System. As you will see, it is possible to connect the Atlantic View Trail with the Salt Marsh and the Shearwater Flyer and continue all the way back into the urban centre.

Cross the highway — there is no crosswalk — and follow the crushed-stone-covered Atlantic View Trail as it heads westward away from the beach. Lawrencetown Lake is to the right, while the drumlin hill forming Lawrencetown Head is on the left.

The path begins as a wide causeway crossing the lake. You are briefly shielded by vegetation once it reaches the side of the drumlin, where an old fence indicates the boundary of former pasturelands. To the right, good views of the marshes are possible. Just before the trail becomes a causeway again, you will pass a Trans Canada Trail Discovery Panel, about the red fox, to your right.

At 3.5 km (2.2 mi), you reach the second causeway section. Highway 207 is visible to your left, and you can see that the trail and road are

Hypothermia

Teeth chattering? Shivering uncontrollably? Hands numb? You may be entering Stage 1 Hypothermia and be in danger. Hypothermia is a condition in which a person's temperature drops below that required for normal metabolism and bodily functions, and it can happen in spring and fall as well as winter. If you experience these symptoms, end your hike immediately. If you are far away from the trailhead, a mildly hypothermic person can be effectively rewarmed through close body contact and by drinking warm, sweet liquids.

rapidly converging. You cross over the decked and railed Lawrencetown Bridge 300 m/yd later. Expect to see a wide variety of birdlife working the shallow waters and mud flats nearby. About 200 m/yd further on, the trail intersects the road once more, and a barricade prevents motorized vehicles from proceeding. The Atlantic View continues straight, but I suggest you turn left and follow the highway for 250 m/yd until you cross its bridge over the Lawrencetown Lake outflow.

Once across the bridge, just in front of the community sign for East Lawrencetown, carefully cross the highway and walk along the sandy bank of the stream, following the water's edge as the outflow curves toward the ocean 300 m/yd away. At low tide a large sand shelf is exposed, but at high tide, the water climbs almost to the large, rocky cobble near the vegetation boundary. Named Stoney Beach, this area extends back toward a grassy hill, Lawrencetown Head, on top of which sits MacDonald's Tea Room and Cake Shop, open only during the summer months.

Follow the beach until you sight a parking area just beyond the rocky cobble. At the eastern end of the lot, a distinct but slender footpath climbs the Lawrencetown Head drumlin, following the edge of slope, and passing close to the Tea

Room. You will notice several small crosses, memorials to the many drowning victims on these beautiful but dangerous beaches. From the top of Lawrencetown Head, the view is tremendous, including the eastern approaches to Halifax Harbour and much of both Stoney Beach and Conrad Beach, which is on the west side of the Lawrencetown River.

Descending on the Lawrencetown Beach side, the trail enters a thick and weather-beaten stand of white spruce trees. Several distinct, though somewhat rugged, paths work through the vegetation and emerge at the bottom of the drumlin by the highway. A footpath parallels the guardrail until it returns to the parking lot where your walk began.

Cellphone Coverage: Good throughout.

Cautionary Notes: Road crossings. High waves and winds during and after storms.

Barrier Beaches

While most beaches are deposits of new sediment constantly reworked and consolidated by the action of waves, the large barrier beaches at Clam Bay, Lawrencetown, and Martinique are composed mainly of material that accumulated during glaciation rather than of new sands produced by the erosion of nearby headlands.

All barrier beaches go through a cycle of erosion, failure, and rebuilding due to their constant landward migration caused by wave and storm action. Martinique is about to fail. In recent years, washovers have occurred regularly, and the dunes that stabilize the beach show high rates of erosion. Sand blowing from the beach is killing other vegetation, resulting in its replacement by dune grass, which does not hold as securely.

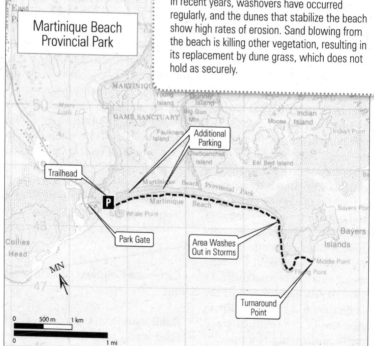

Martinique Beach Provincial Park

Martinique Beach Provincial Park

Length: 9 km (5.5 mi) return
Hiking Time: 2-3 hrs
Type of Trail: cobbled beach,
    natural surface, sandy beach,
Uses: walking, snowshoeing
Facilities: changing rooms,
    outhouses, tables, water
Rating (1-3): 2
Trailhead GPS: N 44° 41' 24.1"
    W 63° 08' 37.8"

Access Information: From Dartmouth, drive east along Highway 107 and Highway 7 to Musquodoboit Harbour, approximately 40 km (25 mi). Turn right onto the road to East Petpeswick and Martinique Beach. Drive 12 km (7.5 mi). The park entrance is on the left less than 200 m/ yd before the road ends.

Outline: Martinique is much like any beach stroll, except that the waves are often exceptionally powerful and loud, particularly during fall storms or offshore hurricanes, when they can break over the dunes. Ascertain what weather conditions are forecast before you begin, especially if you plan to hike as far as Bayers

Islands. The spray here always fogs my glasses, so I recommend wearing contact lenses if you have them (or practise your squinting).

Martinique Beach gets relatively few visitors due to its distance from Halifax and its bitterly cold water. However, the Martinique Beach Game Sanctuary is located in the salt marshes abutting the beach, and birders arrive in substantial numbers in spring and fall to observe the thousands of migrating ducks and geese.

The endangered piping plover regularly nests on the sands of Martinique Beach. It is vital to keep pets on their leash at all times.

Brief Description: When the park is open, you can drive for almost 1.5 km (1 mi) behind the dunes before reaching the final parking area. Several boardwalks and distinct paths lead through the beach grasses to the beach. Those preferring a longer walk should start at the first parking area, just beyond the gate. Most park services can be found here.

Martinique Beach looking toward Whale Point.

Watch for these signs, particularly in the spring.

A rocky promontory known as Whale Point extrudes near the west boundary of the park. Beyond it, white sand stretches for nearly 4 km (2.5 mi) before ending at the Bayers Islands. This sandy shelf is broad and easy walking, especially at low tide. A high wall of grass-covered dunes separates the two sides of the narrow sandy barrier, hiding the marshes on the interior from your view.

About 2.5 km (1.5 mi) from the park entrance, you encounter a small rocky area similar to, but not nearly as distinct as, Whale Point. Past this point the dunes almost disappear, marking where storm surges frequently break through the barrier beach. Winds scour this area and sweep sand far into the shallow waters of Musquodoboit Harbour.

Less than 800 m/yd further on, the beach turns almost 90° to the right toward the Bayers Islands, and walking becomes more challenging. Sand gives way to almost 500 m/yd of rocky cobble that must be crossed before reaching Flying Point, where you find a distinct footpath through the low vegetation. The ocean-facing side of Flying Point is broad coastal barren, while the east side is a solid barrier of white spruce. As you approach the headland of the point, the trees advance to the water's edge and almost prevent further passage. Once around this point, however, it may be warmer than on Martinique Beach. The thick white spruce create a tightly woven blanket of vegetation between you and the wind.

The final stretch crosses the high, steep cobble beach connecting Flying Point to Middle Point. No clear footpath remains beyond the end of the beach connecting these two small knolls. It is possible to continue almost another 1.5 km (1 mi) to

 Piping Plover

For some species, human habits have caused problems. For the piping plover, a small shorebird that lays its eggs in shallow depressions in the sand of beaches above the high tide mark, our fondness for beaches has created disaster. Their small, creamy white speckled eggs are nearly invisible, and are often destroyed quite accidentally by casual strollers or their dogs.

It is believed that fewer than 40 pairs of piping plover still breed along the Atlantic shore and Northumberland Strait, and it is an endangered species. Walkers should be particularly cautious during the breeding season, mid-May to the end of June. Keep dogs on leash, walk below the high tide mark, and possibly consider waiting for a different time of the year to hike along a sandy beach.

Bayers Point, but walking becomes increasingly difficult. I recommend that most people turn around at the end of the path at Flying Point, or once they reach the end of the cobble beach at Middle Point.

Cellphone Coverage: None.

Cautionary Notes: High waves during and after storms. During high tides water can separate Bayers Islands from the main beach.

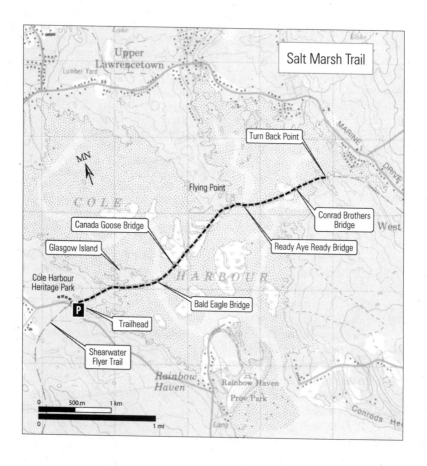

Salt Marsh Trail

MN

Turn Back Point

Flying Point

Conrad Brothers Bridge

Canada Goose Bridge

Ready Aye Ready Bridge

Glasgow Island

West

Cole Harbour Heritage Park

HARBOUR

COLE

Bald Eagle Bridge

P

Trailhead

Shearwater Flyer Trail

Rainbow Haven

Rainbow Haven Prov Park

Camp

Conrods He

0   500 m   1 km

0   1 mi

Salt Marsh Trail

Length: 8 km (5 mi) return
Hiking Time: 2 hrs
Type of Trail: crushed stone
Uses: hiking, biking, snowshoeing,
  cross-country skiing
Facilities: benches, covered picnic
  tables, garbage cans, interpretive
  panels
Rating (1-3): 2
Trailhead GPS: N 44° 39' 26.9"
  W 63° 26' 53.7"

Access Information: From the intersection of Highway 207 with Highway 111 near Penhorn Mall, take
207 for 5 km (3 mi) to Bissett Road.
Turn right onto Bissett and drive for
3.5 km (2.2 mi). A parking area is on
the left.

Outline: The Salt Marsh Trail is
one of the most popular and beautiful coastal walks available in Nova
Scotia. Considering the abundant
natural beauty of Nova Scotia, that
might seem like an unsupportable
claim, yet those who walk the route
regularly will stoutly defend their
assertion against any opposition.
And they have reason to boast. The

Salt Marsh Trail is unlike any other
route in the province because, for
most of its length, it runs along a
slender causeway, ocean water lap-
ping at both sides. It is easy to see
how one can fall in love with it.

This walk is a birder's paradise.
Herons, shorebirds, ducks, geese,
and more than a hundred other

Whistle

Lost? Injured? Cellphone not
working? Carry a whistle. It is
louder and easier to hear than
your voice, and it is less tiring to
blow than to scream. I carry mine
clipped to the strap of my pack.

Camera

I always carry a camera with me
when I hike, and I have captured
some amazing moments of natural
beauty. With modern digital
technology, relatively affordable
cameras produce high quality still
images and even videos. Pictures
are indispensable for enhancing
memories of outstanding scenery.

species can be viewed from this embankment. Virtually no houses can be seen, except for the buildings around Rainbow Haven. Almost all the abutting area is crown land and protected from urban development. Dawn and sunset are particularly attractive times to walk this remarkable section of the Trans Canada Trail.

Brief Description: From the parking lot, follow the wide, crushed-stone pathway past the protective gate and trailhead pavilion. For the first 600 m/yd, you pass through thickly wooded terrain, emerging suddenly to stunningly beautiful coastal views. From here, your route is along a causeway, a former rail bed bisecting the extensive Cole Harbour Salt Marsh.

Barely 200 m/yd later, the causeway touches on a tiny island. A minuscule side footpath, Rosemary's Way, traces its coastline. You will find a bench to sit and enjoy the view of the narrow passage between the trail and nearby Glasgow Island, which is frequented by several species of diving birds. After another 200 m/yd, you reach another tiny island, where the 1 km (0.6 mi) marker is found. Also found on this island are a large informational pavilion, outhouses, and a covered picnic table.

The first bridge, named the Bald Eagle, is in sight barely 100 m/yd away. But before you reach it, you pass a bronze plaque, situated to your left, which tells you that the salt marsh is the Peter McNab Kuhn Conservation Area. Once across the bridge, there is a Trans Canada Trail Discovery Panel — about herons, oddly, not eagles — and another bench.

For the next 1.4 km (0.9 mi), your route follows the exposed, often wind-whipped causeway across the shallow salt marsh until you reach the tip of Flying Point. At low tide, extensive grassy areas are exposed; do not be tempted to walk there without hip waders, however. En route, you cross over the Canada Goose Bridge, pass the 2 km (1.25 mi) marker, and encounter another discovery panel, this one on roses.

After curving past Flying Point, the trail crosses two more bridges: the Ready Aye Ready, so named to commemorate the contributions of the Canadian Forces Naval Construction Troop (Atlantic) who built it, and the Conrad Brothers, who donated a considerable amount of the heavy equipment required to rebuild all four bridges after they were destroyed by Hurricane Juan. You also pass the 3 km (2 mi) marker. This section might also be rougher walking than earlier segments.

Trans Canada Trail

One of the most exciting recreational developments in the world is the construction of a nation-wide, multi-use pathway connecting all ten provinces and three territories. A branch through Truro connects the Halifax-Dartmouth metropolitan area with the main Nova Scotia route of the trail that runs from Amherst to North Sydney.

The Dartmouth Multi-use Trail is part of the Trans Canada Trail system, which will eventually exceed 18,000 km (10,000 mi) when completed. Several other trails profiled in this book, such as the Shearwater Flyer, the Salt Marsh, and portions of the Admiral Lake Loop and Lawrencetown Beach routes are also part of the Trans Canada Trail Network.

At 3.8 km (2.4 mi), the causeway reaches the mainland. Although the Salt Marsh Trail continues an additional 2.5 km (1.6 mi), I suggest continuing only another 200 m/yd. Here you reach another short land bridge over a tiny arm of the marsh, where it is often sheltered from the wind. This can be a pleasant location to rest, enjoy a snack, and then retrace your route back to the trailhead.

Cellphone Coverage: Good throughout.

Cautionary Notes: High waves and winds during and after storms.

A view of Glasgow Island

Shearwater Flyer

Length: East Section — 10 km (6.25 mi) return
West Section — 7 km (4.4 mi) return
Hiking Time: 2-3 hrs each
Type of Trail: crushed stone
Uses: walking, biking, ATVs, snowshoeing, cross-country skiing
Facilities: benches, dog waste bags, garbage cans, interpretive panels
Rating (1-3): 2
Trailhead GPS: N 44° 37' 34.1" W 63° 28' 57.4"

Access Information: From the Mic-Mac Parclo, drive southeast along Highway 111 for 4.7 km (2.9 mi). Turn left onto Pleasant Street, which turns into Main Road, and follow it for 3.4 km (2.1 mi), turning left at Hines Road. Continue for 2.9 km (1.8 mi), turning right onto Caldwell Road. Turn left into a large parking area 250 m/yd later: 1340 Caldwell Road.

Metro Transit Route 60 stops at the junction of Caldwell and Horn roads, 800 m/yd from the trailhead. It also stops on Main Road and Swordfish Drive, 50 m/yd from the end of the west section of the trail.

Outline: Abandoned rail lines converted into recreational pathways, such as the Shearwater Flyer, are often named for their most prominent natural feature. Examples within the Halifax Regional Municipality include the Salt Marsh Trail, the Musquodoboit Rail Trail (named after the river), and the St. Margaret's Bay Rails to Trails. But I have never found anywhere else in the world where a trail has been named for a football club.

In the case of the Shearwater Flyer Trail, as its route skirts the edge of the large Shearwater Air Base for the first third of its length, recognition of this facility's important role in the community is warranted and obvious. However, few would also know that the base organized a Canadian-style football team that competed locally and regionally from 1947 to 1967. Originally named the Dartmouth Air Station Flyers, they later changed their name to the Shearwater Flyers and went on to win a national amateur football championship in 1957. So perhaps, giving the name of a sports team to an enduring recreational facility so close to where they played is quite perfect.

Brief Description: East Section: From the parking area, where a trailhead pavilion features a map, walk to the rail trail and turn right. There is a mileage marker, which indicates that you are at "Km 0" and that it is 5 km (3.1 mi) in the direction you are heading. The trail is very wide, and surfaced in crushed stone. For the entire length, thick vegetation grows on both sides of the pathway.

The trail begins in a 250 m/yd straightaway, giving way to a long, gradual curve left. At 450 m/yd, you pass directly beneath the approach to one of Shearwater's runways, almost the only part of this section with views off the trail. At 600 m/yd, you cross over the De Said Lake Bridge.

This is a pleasant sylvan walk, with an excellent surface that remains dry as the railway was constructed slightly above the surrounding countryside. At the 1 km (0.6 mi) marker, there is a bench, but no view, and after a few snaking, but gradual, turns, the trail settles into a long — very long, more than 1.5 km (0.9 mi) — straightaway 600 m/yd later. While plodding along, you will encounter the Morris Lake Bridge, with a nice view of the open meadow, and the Bissett Lake Bridge, where there is a bench. And just before the "3 km" marker, there is a bench on your right overlooking a tranquil-looking pond that is dynamically vibrant in the spring and summer.

Once past the pond, the trail starts a long curve to the left. For the remainder of the hike you remain bracketed by mainly softwood forests. You might notice some houses on your left, at about 4.6 km (2.9 mi). This is an indication you have nearly completed this section, and within a few hundred metres/yards, you reach Bissett Road, opposite the Salt Marsh Trailhead. Retrace your route to return to your car.

* * *

West Section: This is a very different type of experience from the West Section. Turning left on the rail trail, you almost immediately encounter the first of many road crossings. As with all of them, it is unsigned for automobiles and there is no crosswalk, so be very cautious. Once across, you enter a wooded area, but the vegetation is low and stunted, and there are extensive ATV tracks to your left. As a result, you can always see much further than in the heavily wooded West Section.

At 900 m/yd, the trail crosses a

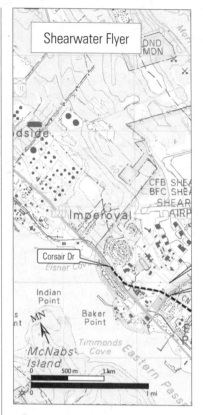

Shearwater Flyer

small, unnamed bridge, and 100 m/yd later, you pass a large oil tank on your left. For the next 1 km (0.6 mi), you pass alongside the former refinery and the carport. At times, hundreds of new cars are parked just on the other side of the fence awaiting shipment. You will also have views of the Eastern Passage and Lawlor Island, just off shore. At 2 km (1.25 mi), the trail crosses Howard Avenue, and 500 m/yd further, it crosses Hines Road.

Now the route moves into a vast open area. To your right is the entrance for the Shearwater Air Base, and the trail crosses Bonaventure Avenue less than 30 m/yd from the security gate. For the next 600 m/yd, the trail stays in the open, passing among buildings associated with the base, including the school and the gymnasium. With Main Road approaching on your left, you enter a small patch of forest for the final

200 m/yd, the trail ending at Corsair Drive, where there is a trailhead pavilion. To return to the Caldwell Road trailhead, retrace your steps.

Cellphone Coverage: Good throughout.

Cautionary Notes: Motorized use, poison ivy, road crossings.

Willowdale

Bissett Lake

Salt Marsh Trail

Bisset Road

R1 30,
Cole Harbour
IR 30

Morris Lake

De Said Lake

Bench by Pond

Morris Lake Bridge

Bisset Lake Bridge

SHEARWATER AIRPORT

ARWATER
EARWATER
RWATER
PORT

SHEARWATER

Shearwater Main Gate

BFC SHEARWATER

De Said Lake Bridge

East Section

Hines Road

Road Crossing

Howard Ave

P

Trailhead

West Section

astern
assage

Flare Stack 114
Waste
Petroleum Refinery

Mobile Home Park

Mobile Home
Hall

Smelt

322

Mobile Ho

Bisset Lake Bridge, Shearwater Flyer

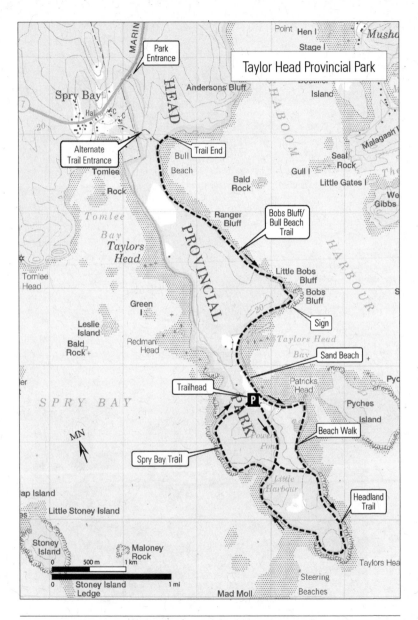

Taylor Head Provincial Park

Park Entrance

Spry Bay

Andersons Bluff

Alternate Trail Entrance

Tomlee

Rock

Trail End

Bull Beach

Bald Rock

Ranger Bluff

Bobs Bluff/ Bull Beach Trail

Tomlee Bay

Taylors Head

PROVINCIAL

Little Bobs Bluff

Bobs Bluff

Sign

Tomlee Head

Green I

Leslie Island

Bald Rock

Redman Head

Taylors Head Bay

Sand Beach

Trailhead

SPRY BAY

Patricks Head

Pyches Island

Beach Walk

Spry Bay Trail

PARK

Power Pond

Little Harbour

Headland Trail

MN

ap Island

Little Stoney Island

Stoney Island

Maloney Rock

Taylors Hea

0   500 m   1 km

0   1 mi

Stoney Island Ledge

Mad Moll

Steering Beaches

Point Hen I   Musho

Stage I

Boutilier Island

HABOOM

Seal Rock

Gull I   Little Gates I

HARBOUR

The

We Gibbs

Taylor Head Provincial Park

Length: Beach Walk — 2 km (1.25 mi) return
Bobs Bluff/Bull Beach — 9.5 km (6 mi) return
Headland — 7 km (4.4 mi) return
Spry Bay — 3.5 km (2.25 mi) return

Hiking Time: 45 min-4 hrs

Type of Trail: beach, natural surface, rock

Uses: walking, snowshoeing, cross-country skiing

Facilities: change houses, garbage cans, interpretive panels, outhouses, picnic tables, water

Rating (1-3): Beach Walk — 1, Bobs Bluff/Bull Beach, Headland— 3, Spry Bay— 2

Trailhead GPS: N 44° 50' 39.5" W 62° 34' 51.4" (Park Entrance)

Access Information: The park is near Spry Bay, address 20140 Highway 7, 100 km (62 mi) from Halifax and 11 km (7 mi) from Sheet Harbour. A very large sign marks the entrance; turn onto the dirt road and drive 5 km (3 mi) to the parking lot. Hikers should continue to the final (4th)

Song Sparrow

area; wheelchair access to the beach is available from the first lot.

Alternate access to the Bobs Bluff/ Bull Beach Trails is found 800 m/yd down the park road from the park entrance..

Outline: Situated on the rugged eastern shore, Taylor Head is a narrow granite finger jutting more than 6.5 km (4 mi) into the Atlantic Ocean. With more than 16 km (10 mi) of coastline, of which at least 1 km (0.6 mi) is magnificent white sand beach and approximately 18 km (11.25 mi) of trails, this is a wonderful spot to hike. Radiating out from a central

GPS/Compass

Nothing has revolutionized wilderness travel recently as much as Global Positioning System satellite navigation. With a GPS unit, you can travel directly to any location for which you have the coordinates. I use one but also carry a compass as a backup; it has no batteries to go dead.

Map

Hiking without a map is like walking with one eye closed. What is the name of that lake? How high is that hill? How much further do I have to walk? With a map, you have answers to all those questions, an indispensable guide to your surroundings, and an important safety tool.

start at the 4th parking area, at least four options are available. As your start is adjacent to the beach and the picnic area, there will be ample opportunity to shuck the pack and relax.

The trails on Taylor Head are narrow and occasionally challenging. Novices should try the shorter routes before attempting the Headland or Bull Beach sections. Experienced hikers will prefer to complete the entire network. Take time to read

all the many interpretive panels found near the start and to visit Newcombe's Graveyard.

Taylor Head extends far into the Atlantic and experiences high winds and extreme conditions much of the year. Users of the Headland Trail in particular should expect lower temperatures and should avoid the ocean's edge in stormy and high-water conditions.

Brief Description: The shortest hike is the Beach Walk. A 2 km (1.25 mi) return trip, it begins on the sand on Psyche Cove and follows the coastline onto a barrier beach system separating a sheltered pond from Mushaboom Harbour. The hike originally ended at the vegetation, but the narrow stream once separating the cobbled beach from the peninsula has filled in, and it is possible to connect with the Headland Trail. An easy walk, ideal for birdwatching, as several species of duck are commonly found in the pond.

Next are the Spry Bay and Headland trails. In the form of a stacked loop, these can be undertaken either as a 3.5 km (2.25 mi) or 7 km (4.5 mi) hike. My favourite, this path takes you to the very tip of Taylor Head with its rocky coastline and windswept barrens. I recommend following the eastern boundary initially, crossing the remnants of the

Bandana

One of the more useful small items you can carry, bandanas make great headbands and neck protection. They can even substitute for a hat to provide shade from the sun. During hot weather, soaking your bandana and wetting your hair and face is almost as refreshing as a cool drink, and I regularly use mine to wipe acrid perspiration from my eyes. They take no space and weigh nothing: carry two!

abandoned fields cleared by early settlers and hugging the inside of the pond.

After 1 km (0.6 mi), a junction permits cutting across the narrow peninsula to the western coast and following the shorter loop back to the start area. There are frequent lookoffs facing Spry Bay, and although the walking is rough at times, substantial construction works, such as stairs and bridges, make it possible for most people to complete this trail comfortably.

Turning left adds 3.5 km (2.25 mi) to the walk but is well worth the extra effort. Once past the pond, the trail hugs the rocky shore protected by the stunted coastal forest. Reaching the headland, the krummholz (see p. 123) gives way to barrens: rocky open lands created by the harsh climate and wretched soil. Only stunted spruce, larch, juniper, and lichens resist the high winds and fog. The trail almost disappears here and on the rocky, cobbled beaches

Lookoff along the Spry Bay Trail, Taylor Head Provincial Park

on the western shore. Rugged and rough, this is a wonderfully scenic hike.

Bobs Bluff/Bull Beach will give you the longest walk in the park, almost 9.5 km (6 mi). Turn left at the parking area and follow the main beach to its northern end, where a sign and map indicate the start of the footpath. Narrow and windy, rising and falling as it hugs the uneven coast, this is a hiker's dream. Frequent viewing spots on high bluffs afford vistas of Taylors Head Bay. At Bobs Bluff, watch the water for seals watching you. The 3 km (2 mi) path to Bull Beach follows the eastern shore as it gently curves to the slender neck at the base of Taylor Head. An inland-facing lookoff surveys an excellent example of a raised bog with peaty soil. Reaching tiny Bull Beach and the end of the trail, retrace your route to return to the start area. You are less than 200 m/yd from the road, which provides an alternative return route.

Cellphone Coverage: Good throughout.

Cautionary Notes: Animals. High waves during and after storms. Rugged terrain.

CENTRAL – SOUTH SHORE

Oakfield Provincial Park

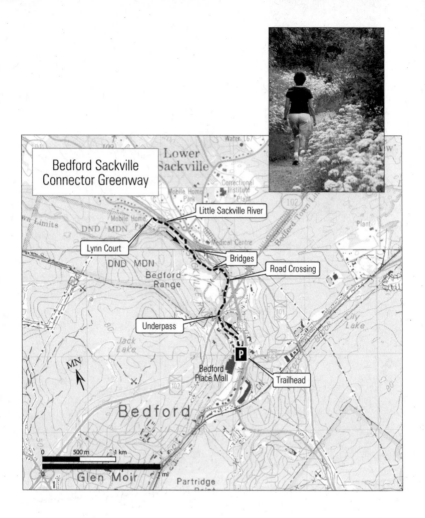

Bedford Sackville
Connector Greenway

Little Sackville River

Lynn Court

Bridges

Road Crossing

Underpass

Bedford
Place Mall

Trailhead

MN

500 m   1 km

Bedford

Glen Moir   Partridge

Bedford Sackville Connector Greenway

Length: 5 km (3 mi) return
Hiking Time: 1+ hr
Type of Trail: crushed stone
Uses: walking, biking, snow-shoeing, cross-country skiing
Facilities: benches, garbage cans, interpretive panels
Rating (1-3): 1
Trailhead GPS: N 44° 38' 37.1"
    W 63° 20' 56.6"

Access Information: From Highway 102, take Exit 4A/4B onto Highway 1 in the direction of Bedford. Drive 800 m/yd to the intersection with River Lane. Turn right at the streetlight, cross the bridge over the Sackville River, and proceed into the Bedford Place Mall parking area. Take the first available right, toward the True North Diner. A pedestrian bridge is in the northern corner of the parking lot.

Metro Transit routes 66, 80, 82, and 89 stop on Bedford Highway approximately 250 m/yd from the trailhead.

Outline: Known as the "Original Main Street" of Bedford, the Sackville River in the spring enjoys impressive runs of gaspereau, eel, sea trout, and even the occasional Atlantic salmon. The Bedford Sackville Connector Greenway revives the role of the river as a transportation artery, providing almost the only legal route for pedestrians and cyclists to travel between the two communities.

A great deal of effort has been made to develop this trail into a safe walking route in the narrow corridor remaining between river, two multi-lane highways, and an active Department of National Defence complex. Yet despite its occasional claustrophobic confinements, there are two or three sections of remarkably attractive natural surroundings,

and it makes for a very pleasant short walk. In particular, watch for trumpeter swans, in the river near Bedford Place Mall.

Brief Description: Cross the excellent steel footbridge over the Sackville River. The path on the other side is wide and covered in crushed stone. The path curves left and follows the (usually) gently flowing river, which is lined with thick vegetation. Plant and bird people should particularly enjoy this section as you pass through a lovely area of alders, wild roses, Queen Anne's lace, and virgin's bower. Numerous warblers flirt in and out of view, enticing you to loiter in the hope of a better glimpse.

Less than 200 m/yd later, you reach Range Park, off to your right, and its large playing fields. This area is floodplain, and walkers during the summer and fall, when the river is low and slow moving, might have difficulty imagining that several times every year this area is underwater. The path skirts the edge of the field and, 550 m/yd into your walk, passes underneath busy, noisy, Highway 102.

On the far side, you will find a sign that welcomes you to the Bedford Sackville Connector Trail and outlines many of its regulations. The path now squeezes itself into the narrow space between the Department of National Defence Firing Range on the left and the multi-lane highway on the right. At 850 m/yd, a narrow, low-ceilinged tunnel passes beneath another road and signs warn cyclists to dismount. (This is so small, it almost looks like a doorway.)

The trail continues, wedged between roads, crossing the next 150

 Ticks

Ticks are small, eight-legged animals related to spiders – not insects – that attach themselves to mammals and gorge themselves on their blood. Unfed ticks are small, not much larger than a sesame seed, and they move around on the ground, grass, and bushes, waiting to attach themselves to any animal that brushes past.

Ticks are found throughout southern Nova Scotia, and their range is spreading into the Halifax Regional Municipality as the climate changes. Most tick bites cause only skin irritation and swelling, but a small percentage of ticks carry other diseases, although the worst, Lyme disease, has not been found in ticks in Nova Scotia.

DEET on clothes is effective at repelling ticks, but other measures are prudent. For more information on ticks, go to http://health.gov.on.ca/english/public/pub/disease/lyme_mn.html.

---

m/yd later. A gate limits access to the path, and there is a stop sign posted for trail users. Once across, the trail begins a long, sweeping curve to the left. Multi-lane Highway 101 is now to your right, but a small wooded hill rises on your left. After 350 m/yd, you reach another impressive bridge crossing the Sackville River. A posted sign reminds you of your proximity to the firing range. There is no danger while on the trail, but you may find the sound of continuous and often rapid gunfire disconcerting.

Once across the bridge, the path turns right, paralleling the river, bordered on your left by a high fence. This is the most attractive section of the walk, capped by many mature trees and dotted with benches next to the water's edge. After 400 m/yd, you pass beneath power lines, then the trail briefly curves left up a small hill and slightly away from the river, before swinging right and dropping back down to another bridge over the river, 2 km (1.25 mi) from the start.

Once again, the trail is sandwiched, highway to the right and river to the left. It continues so for another 300 m/yd, crossing one very small bridge en route to the larger structure crossing the Little Sackville River, which feeds from the right. An interpretive panel here tells about the efforts made to

Call of Nature

No, not a wolf howl. When you do need to … "s**t in the woods," remember that the trail is a public place. Move well off the path, stay 25 m\yd away from water, and if you can, dig a scat hole. When finished, cover it up. Because the chemicals used in their production will leach into the soil, sanitary napkins, tampons, disposable diapers, and toilet paper should be packed out.

improve fish habitat along the Sackville River.

Only 200 m/yd remain. The trail turns away from the Sackville River and makes its way along a road embankment with extensive wooden fencing on the downslope side. It ends at the sidewalk at the junction of Lynn Court and Old Sackville Road. If you turn right and continue along the street for 400 m/yd, you will reach the Fultz House Museum in Sackville. Otherwise, retrace your route back to the start.

Cellphone Coverage: Good throughout.

Cautionary Notes: Road crossing, narrow tunnel.

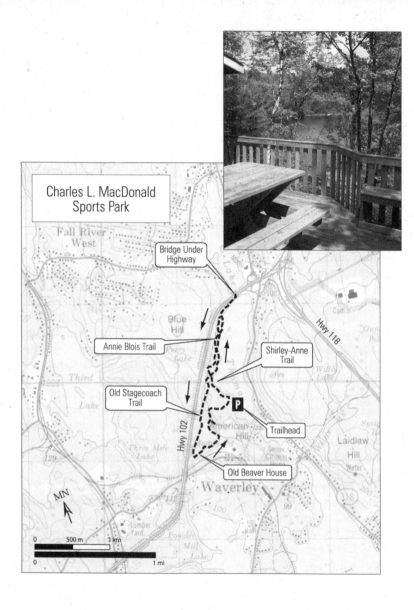

Charles L. MacDonald
Sports Park

Fall River
West

Bridge Under
Highway

Blue
Hill

Annie Blois Trail

Shirley-Anne
Trail

Old Stagecoach
Trail

P

Trailhead

Old Beaver House

Hwy 118

Hwy 102

American
Hill

Laidlaw
Hill

Waverley

MN

0   500 m   1 km

0   1 mi

Third
Lake

Three Mile
Lake

Lumber
Yard

Powder
Mill
Lake

Charles L. MacDonald Sports Park

Length: 6 km (3.75 mi) return
Hiking Time: 2 hrs
Type of Trail: natural surface, crushed stone
Uses: walking, biking, snowshoeing, cross-country skiing
Facilities: benches, garbage cans, outhouse, picnic tables
Rating (1-3): 2
Trailhead GPS: N 44° 47' 29" W 63° 36' 38.4"

Access Information: From Highway 102, take Exit 4C toward Lower Sackville. Approximately 1.5 km (1 mi) later, you will reach the Cobequid Road, where you turn right. Follow the Cobequid Road for 5.5 km (3.5 mi). Turn left onto the first gravel road after the railway track crossing; watch for a sign marking the Charles L. MacDonald Sports Park, 1390 Cobequid Road. Continue on the gravel track to a gate 400 m/yd from the turnoff; the parking lot is reached 500 m/yd later.

The park is open from 8:00 a.m. to 8:00 p.m.

Outline: The Charles L. MacDonald Sports Park is a wonderful network of wide, well-maintained trails near Waverley, situated in a narrow strip of wooded land bounded by Highway 102 and Lake Thomas. This park, the property of the Waverley Amateur Athletic Association, contains rolling hills, considerable lake frontage, and attractive hardwood and softwood stands. The property also contains a large pond that is home to frogs and salamanders, many bird species, a family of beavers, and at least one kind of turtle.

The trailhead and parking area look rather rough and unpromising, which might lead you to imagine that the trails are similarly unprepossessing. However, once you begin your walk, you will soon discover otherwise.

Brief Description: Start to the right of the green shed, where there is a bench, on the Shirley-Anne Trail. This is wide, like an old road, and is pleasantly shaded by a high canopy of trees. It meanders along the

descents. It is a good walk for young children and those with limited mobility.

Three times you will encounter junctions with paths leading to the interior; keep right, until you reach a T-junction at about 1.5 km (0.9 mi). A sign indicates that the Annie Blois Trail heads to the left. Again keep right, now on a path surfaced in crushed stone. With the sounds of busy Highway 102 growing constantly louder, this trail continues to parallel Lake Thomas for another 350 m/yd, until it reaches the bridge where Highway 102 crosses the lake. A narrow, low-ceilinged bridge crosses underneath the highway. On the far side you will find a number of informal footpaths heading off into the forest, but the managed trail ends. There is, however, an attractive little cove that is an ideal spot for a swim on a hot summer day.

Return to the T-junction, having walked 2.3 km (1.4 mi). Return along the Annie Blois Trail, which is much hillier and more challenging than the Shirley-Anne. It is also less well-maintained, and features a natural surface. This heads inland, closer to the highway, working up and down the hillside, with some occasionally steep climbs on a deeply eroded path. Although no uphill is more than a few hundred metres/yards long, some will find them more

shore of Lake Thomas, mostly on a natural surface of compacted earth, with occasional patches of crushed stone. You will come across numerous planters containing small shrubs and trees, several picnic tables, and benches situated in tiny coves or on small hills perched above the water. The Shirley-Anne Trail is relatively level, with a few minor climbs and

Beaver House Trail

 Beaver

While walking near lakes, you may notice low mounds of mud and dead branches in shallow water. These are beaver lodges, the homes of Canada's most popular rodent. If startled, beavers will slap the water with their tails as a warning signal and dive underwater, remaining submerged for up to 15 minutes.

Their incisor teeth never stop growing, so beavers must constantly be gnawing things to wear them down. This makes them unpopular neighbours for people living near lakes or streams who plant ornamental trees.

Beavers energetically construct elaborate structures such as lodges and dams to regulate the level of the water. They abandon an area when their food supply of nearby poplar, willow, birch, and alder is depleted.

Mayflower

The mayflower is a welcome signal that spring is just around the corner. Appearing in mid-April, the tiny blooms vary from almost pure white to rich pink, and disappear by mid-May. Well-drained, acidic soils suit this fragrant flower best, and it can be discovered in barrens, woods, or open pastures, its blossoms nearly hidden under old leaves or in tall grass.

Also known as trailing arbutus, and found throughout the province, the mayflower was chosen to be the floral emblem of Nova Scotia in 1901. Mayflowers range from Labrador to Florida, and related species are found in Japan, Asia Minor, and the Caucasus Mountains.

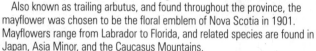

challenging than they wish, and may prefer to return along the shore path. At each junction keep right, following the Annie Blois until you reach the junction with the Karen Furneaux Trail and the Old Stagecoach Trail, at about 3.3 km (2.1 mi).

Take the latter, keeping right and heading uphill again on the beautiful, grassy treadway. The Old Stagecoach Trail roughly parallels Highway 102 for almost 1 km (0.6 mi). It passes through some beautiful oak and occasional stands of hemlock on a grass-covered treadway before turning sharply and descending to the edge of the small pond on the opposite side from the entry road. Near this end of the park, around the Cobequid Road, the property is much wider, and there is room for more routes.

Old Stagecoach Trail gives way to Big Paul's Loop. This finally curves left and returns alongside a wet area, where a 100 m/yd boardwalk, named the Old Beaver House Trail, conducts you to a small island with views of both old and new beaver activity. From here, the trail traces the dry edge of this low and sometimes boggy area. At the junction with the Anne Dodge Trail, keep right; it will return you to the parking area.

Cellphone Coverage: Good throughout.

Cautionary Notes: None.

Crystal Crescent Beach Provincial Park

Length: 4 km (2.5 mi) return
Hiking Time: 1 hr
Type of Trail: sand beaches, former roads, walking paths, boardwalk
Uses: walking, snowshoeing
Facilities: garbage cans, outhouses
Rating (1-3): 2
Trailhead GPS: N 44° 27' 40.7"
   W 63° 37' 05.6"

Access Information: From the Armdale Rotary in Halifax, take Herring Cove Road, Highway 349, through the village of Sambro, about 20 km (12.5 mi). Follow the narrow, twisty road until you sight signs indicating the route to Crystal Crescent Beach. Several junctions must be navigated correctly in the next 3 km (2 mi), including turning right at a gated entrance, and the last 500 m/yd are along a potholed gravel road. Park in the first lot. The park gate closes at 8:00 p.m.

Outline: This is one of my favourite walks, and I have been coming here for more than 30 years. Local hiking clubs, field naturalists, and birders have long recognized the special

nature of this tiny finger of exposed coastal headland so close to Halifax. Crystal Crescent remained largely untouched until the late 1990s, when the trail was developed.

You cannot start a walk with a better view. From the beautiful white sand of Coote Cove, you look across Sambro Harbour to the rugged granite islands defining the western approaches to Halifax Harbour. The red-and-white-striped lighthouse on Sambro Island looks more caricature than real, but it once warned approaching vessels of nearby reefs such as Shag Rock, Mad Rock, and The Sisters. Expect hundreds at Crystal Crescent Beach on summer weekends.

Dune Systems

Dunes are sand deposits on beaches that develop into a series of one or more ridges through wind and wave action, becoming stabilized by the growth of American beach grass. These fragile grasses that populate the dunes are essential to their survival.

All sand beaches have some measure of dune systems, although beaches on the Atlantic coast of the mainland tend to be retreating landward too rapidly for full successional series development. New dune ridges develop on the seaward side depending upon the sediment supply, the pace of erosion, and the rate of sea level rise.

Lawrencetown and other provincial beaches often feature extensive boardwalks to channel human passage that might otherwise quickly kill the stabilizing grass, causing more rapid dune erosion. Please stay on the boardwalks at all times.

The ground away from the beach is wet much of the time, and Pennant Point is often buffeted by high, cool winds. Wear appropriate footwear and clothing. Both during and just after a storm, waves can be substantially higher than normal. Be careful near the water's edge.

Brief Description: At the beach end of the parking lot, a boardwalk cuts through the line of dunes to the right. Either follow the boardwalk or walk along the beach, letting the sand get between your toes. At the far end of this first beach, a small stream empties into the ocean, and a bridge has been constructed to

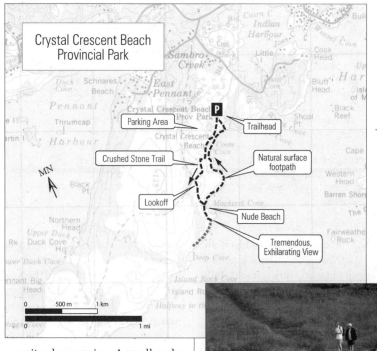

Crystal Crescent Beach
Provincial Park

Parking Area

Trailhead

Crushed Stone Trail

Natural surface
footpath

Lookoff

Nude Beach

Tremendous,
Exhilarating View

MN

0   500 m   1 km

0   1 mi

permit a dry crossing. A small rocky rise separates the two beaches in Coote Cove, and several distinct footpaths lead over it. From the right, paths connecting the newer parking lots on the hill wind down the slope. On the far side of the rise, the boardwalked trail remains in the grasses behind the dunes. Once again, you may decide to walk the sand beach instead.

At the far end of the second beach both routes converge at a modest outflow from a tiny pond at the base of a hill. You have a choice either to continue to follow the coastline or to turn away from the ocean and climb a crushed-stone track up the hillside. I recommend the latter, as you get an increasingly impressive view of Sambro Harbour and the nearby islands as you climb. Just

Nude Beach

A word of warning: for more than 30 years Mackerel Cove has been a nude beach. On hot, sunny summer days as many as 200 nude bathers can be found working on their tans both on the beach and further along Pennant Point. Hardy naturists can be found there as early as April and as late as October.

Although not well accepted in the neighbouring communities, the naturists, many of whom are European immigrants, remove garbage from this beach and organize special events on holidays. The code of conduct at Mackerel Cove beach is no different than you would find on any other public beach in the province, except that most people are unclothed. If this makes you uncomfortable, perhaps you should avoid this beach.

before the crest, 1 km (0.6 mi) from the start, you encounter a junction with an old road. Turn left and walk toward the high ground 60 m/yd away, turning off the old road onto a grassy path almost immediately. From the crest of the hill, where possibly the best view on the walk will be found, continue down the slope to Mackerel Cove and another sandy beach.

The path continues along a boardwalk in the dunes behind the beach. Alternatively, you may walk to the end of the sand beach and climb the pile of rocks for views of the magnificent, rugged coastline beyond. Informal tracks continue, although the maintained trail ends here, 1.5 km (0.9 mi) from the trailhead.

Retrace your path across the beach to the narrow footpath that follows the coastline. This traces the point all the way back to Coote Cove and the junction at the end of the second beach and makes a pleasant, although slightly longer, return walk. On your way, watch for the many coastal plants growing in the low brush along your route. In August, this hillside is a favourite place to pick blueberries.

Cellphone Coverage: Good throughout.

Cautionary Notes: High waves during and after storms. The beach at Mackerel Cove is popular with naturists.

Pennant Point shoreline, Crystal Crescent Beach Provincial Park,
Central – South Shore

Martinique Beach Provincial Park, Eastern Shore

Martinique Beach Provincial Park, Eastern Shore

Krummholz

The effects of high winds and salt spray can be seen in the trees that grow near the ocean, especially those at the edge of barrens. Few species, particularly hardwoods, can survive the massive amounts of salt that are deposited on them by the fogs that roll in from offshore. Almost all the trees found by the ocean edge are the very hardy white spruce.

Fierce Atlantic gales produce a most dramatic visual effect. They stunt and shape the white spruce, causing dense branching that grows in the opposite direction from the prevailing winds. Several trees will cluster together in thick stands, forming a dense curtain of branches that insulates the lee side and protects the walker on a blustery day.

This phenomenon of stunted trees is called "krummholz," from the German word meaning "crooked wood."

Old Stagecoach Trail, Charles L. MacDonald Sports Park, Central–South Shore

Elevated bridge to permit canoes passing,
Old Annapolis Road, Central–South Shore

Polly Cove, Central–South Shore

Pitcher Plant, The Bluff Wilderness Trail – Pot Lake Loop, Central–South Shore

Dollar Lake Provincial Park,
Central–South Shore

Dollar Lake Provincial Park

Length: 8 km (5 mi) return

Hiking Time: 2-3 hrs

Type of Trail: beach, fields, gravel road, natural surface, pavement

Uses: walking, biking, snow-shoeing, cross-country skiing

Facilities: boat launch, campground, canteen, covered tables, garbage cans, outhouses, picnic tables, unsupervised beach, water

Rating (1-3): 2

Trailhead GPS: N 44° 56' 45.9" W 63° 18' 54.2"

Access Information: From Halifax, turn off Highway 102 at Exit 5A. Drive through the Aerotech Business Park looking for the Old Guysborough Road, Highway 212. Continue past the airport and golf course at Goffs for a further 25 km (15.5 km). The park entrance is on your right, although the sign is down during the winter months. Turn off the highway onto a gravel road; a parking area is 50 m/yd in from the pavement.

The approaches to the park are well signed, and you can find your way there from the Eastern Shore along Highway 357 from Musquodoboit Harbour and from Truro along Highways 224 and 277.

Outline: Opened in the mid-1980s, Dollar Lake is almost 1,200 ha (3,000 ac) in area. It contains more than 100 camping sites and is criss-crossed by innumerable logging roads and game trails. There are almost 10 km (6.25 mi) of gravelled road within the park boundaries, permitting a range of walks for all different fitness levels. Much of the park's trail system was extensively damaged in 1993 by Hurricane Juan and has not been reopened.

This can be a pleasant refuge during the fall, when hunting season closes much of the forest to recreational walkers. The route I have described is best used when the park is closed, after Labour Day in September and before the Victoria Day weekend in May.

Dollar Lake is also one of the closest spots to Halifax where people may be reasonably certain to find snow — about double what the urban area

Alder

Nature never sits still, and as soon as humans clear land, plants begin to recolonize the empty space. Several of these pioneer species are alders, shrubs that are common on poorly drained soils, alongside streams, in ditches, and beside roads. Much of the Dollar Lake route will be lined with them.

They have almost no commercial value. However, alders help increase the fertility of nutrient-poor land because they efficiently convert atmospheric nitrogen into nitrates. Wildlife benefits from the shelter thick alder stands provide. Many birds nest in the trees and eat the small, nutlike buds in winter. Snowshoe hare and moose eat the leaves.

The early settlers used alders medicinally, based on recipes they learned from the Mi'kmaq.

receives and longer lasting. Its roads are therefore excellent for cross-country skiing and snowshoeing.

Brief Description: From the gate across the park entrance, the road climbs gradually for 700 m/yd until it reaches the junction for the day-use park and camping areas; continue straight. The road climbs for another 600 m/yd, but once you have reached the highest elevation, it is all downhill for 1 km (0.5 mi) to the picnic grounds. Ignore the many old roads branching from the main track. Just before reaching the lake, the road opens onto a large parking area. On the far side you will notice several buildings: changing rooms, washrooms, and the canteen. The beach and picnic areas are found just beyond.

It is often quite windy by the lake and much cooler. However, the picnic tables are left in the area year-round, so this can be a site for a pleasant lunch if you wish. Once at the beach, turn left and follow the lakeshore. A bridge crosses Dollar Lake Brook and connects to the campground. A family of beavers moved into this area recently, and you can see their lodge from the bridge. On the beach side, there is an area where alder and birch have been nearly all removed; more than 50 small trees have been felled, and their gnawed stumps are everywhere.

On the far side of the bridge, there is a large grassy field with a modern playground and the boat-launching area. From here, you can take the road back to the park entrance, climb a set of stairs into the camping area, or find a small path that follows the shoreline. The footpath rounds a small point, staying in the small fringe of trees separating the campground from the lake. In less than 1 km (0.6 mi), it reaches a

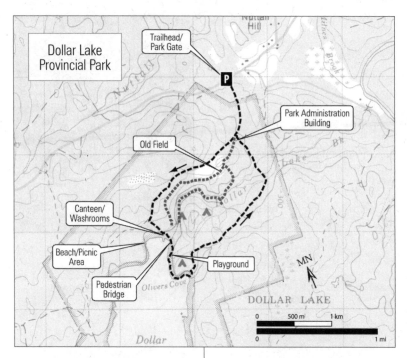

second, much smaller beach area at the mouth of another brook entering Olivers Cove. Although a trail continues further along the lake, there is currently no bridge across the brook. Turn left, at the beach, climbing a set of stairs where you will reach a dirt road. Turn right, and follow it the 3 km (2 mi) back to the park entrance. Make certain to turn right at the first major intersection, following the gravelled track up the hillside.

One worthwhile diversion may be found shortly before reaching the camping/day-use road junction. The remains of a farm, including several fields that are still worked, can be found on a drumlin just behind the park administration buildings. You have a fairly good view of Dollar Lake to the south and the Musquodoboit Valley to the northeast. You will sight the open area on your left, approximately 2.5 km (1.5 mi) from the camping area.

Cellphone Coverage: Good throughout.

Cautionary Notes: Animals.

First and Second Lake Trails

Trail Junction

Second Lake Trail

First Lake Drive

Sack-A-Wa Canoe Club

Playing Fields

Trailhead

First Lake Trail

First and Second Lake Trails

Length: First Lake – 3.8 km (2.4 mi) return

Second Lake – 2.8 km (1.75 mi) return

Hiking Time: 1 hr each

Type of Trail: crushed stone

Uses: walking, biking, snow-shoeing, cross-country skiing

Facilities: benches, dog waste bags, garbage cans, picnic tables

Rating (1-3): 1

Trailhead GPS: N 44° 46' 08.7" W 63° 39' 02.9"

Access Information: From Highway 102, take Exit 4B toward Lower Sackville. Approximately 1.5 km (1 mi) later, you will reach the Cobequid Road, where you turn right. Follow the Cobequid Road for 2.6 km (1.6 mi), then turn left onto First Lake Drive. Continue 600 m/yd; parking is on left.

Metro Transit route 82 stops at Cobequid Road and First Lake Drive, 700 m/yd from the trailhead or at the far end of the First Lake Trail by the Sack-A-Wa Canoe Club, 133 First Lake Drive.

Outline: As housing developments mushroomed in the Lower Sackville-Waverley area in the 1970s, residents became concerned about their rapidly disappearing green spaces, particularly in what was known as the "Sackville Lakes District." This pocket of forested land and relatively pristine lakes had long been used informally for recreation.

The Second Lake Regional Park Association was created to lobby for the area's protection, and in 1999, the province designated 281 ha (694 ac) as a provincial park reserve. In the past several years, the association and the municipal government have begun to develop a series of shared-use trails. Additional routes are planned.

This route description profiles two separate paths: one following the shore of First Lake and the other looping through the forest to Second Lake. However, they share a common trailhead, so you may walk them separately or together.

Brief Description: **First Lake:** From the parking lot, take the crushed-stone pathway on the same side of First Lake Drive. Curving to the right, this broad pathway quickly reaches the lakeshore and, keeping close to it except for a few wet areas, continues through thick forest. The houses of Lower Sackville line the opposite shore.

At 900 m/yd, there are large sports fields to your right, and there are several access connectors. The path continues in the narrow fringe of trees between fields and lake for about 300 m/yd before the fields give way again to forested land. At 1.3 km (0.8 mi), a major connector on the right will take you to First Lake Drive and a bus stop.

The path continues alongside the lake, and there are now occasional benches facing the water. By 300 m/yd later, when you cross a sturdy bridge over a small stream, you will notice that the backyards of the houses on First Lake Drive come all the way down the trail and that many have constructed small docks on the lake. Please be respectful of private property.

Once past the bridge, a further 200 m/yd of attractive forest walking remains before the path curves right for another 100 m/yd, running alongside the Sack-A-Wa Canoe Club, to finish on First Lake Road. Retrace your route back to the trailhead.

***

Second Lake: Cross First Lake Drive and enter the thick forest on a crushed-stone pathway, the entrance narrowed by boulders. There is a trailhead pavilion to the right just past the gates, which, when I visited, featured both regulatory information and announcements but not a map of the system. Initially slightly downhill, the wide path passes through dense vegetation, providing no extended views. Frequent side trails separate from both sides, but as these are not surfaced, your route is easy to follow even though there is no formal signage.

After 500 m/yd, you reach a junction. Turn right, and continue downhill, paralleling a small creek for another 400 m/yd to the shore of Second Lake at a tiny inlet, where there is a picnic table. Remarkably,

Garbage Bag

Always, always pack out your trash. Everything you carry in, you should carry back out. And unless you want to make a mess of your pack, you will probably need a waterproof bag to do so. You might even pick up any other garbage you find along the trail, and make the hike a better experience for the next person.

Porcupine

The porcupine is one of the more easily recognized mammals in Nova Scotia, but so shy as to be rarely encountered in the wild. Dogs, however, show an ingenious ability to locate porcupines and often end up with a snout full of spiny quills.

Famous for its formidable defensive armament, the porcupine is actually a rodent that feeds on the bark of different trees usually high above ground level. In September and October, their mating season, they can be located by their whimpering grunts, usually in the early evening or after dark and sounding quite loud in the quiet forest.

considering how thickly the area is populated, there is almost no sign of human habitation visible from this spot. The trail turns left, following the shore of Second Lake for another 550 m/yd. This is lovely, peaceful walking as the path cuts across the top of a low-lying peninsula and crosses a small brook.

When you reach the next junction there is another picnic table, set to overlook the water. Should you wish, you could continue to follow the lakeshore. About 500 m/yd have been completed, and future plans include extending the trail the additional 1 km (0.6 mi) to Metropolitan Avenue.

However, to return to the trailhead, turn left and work your way up a surprisingly steep hillside for several hundred metres/yards before the trail curves left and gradually lessens in incline. Once again you are enclosed in thick, impenetrable forest. On a wet day, as it was when I walked this path, the branches bow low from the weight of the rain, narrowing the trail corridor.

After walking 800 m/yd from Second Lake, you reach the first junction, completing your loop. Turn right, and the trailhead is 400 m/yd further along.

Cellphone Coverage: Good throughout.

Cautionary Notes: Road crossing.

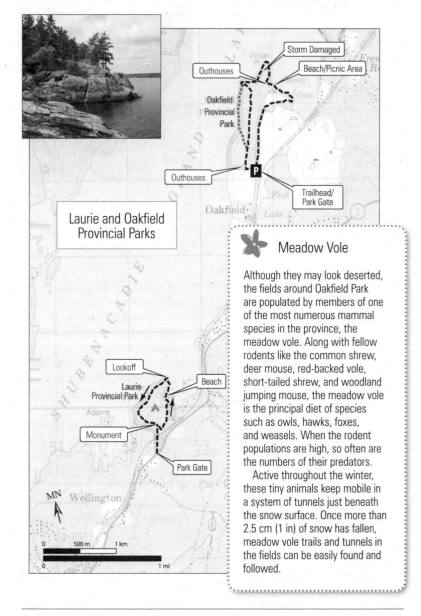

Laurie and Oakfield Provincial Parks

Storm Damaged

Beach/Picnic Area

Outhouses

Oakfield Provincial Park

Outhouses

Trailhead/ Park Gate

Lookoff

Beach

Laurie Provincial Park

Monument

Park Gate

MN

Wellington

0   500 m   1 km

1 mi

Meadow Vole

Although they may look deserted, the fields around Oakfield Park are populated by members of one of the most numerous mammal species in the province, the meadow vole. Along with fellow rodents like the common shrew, deer mouse, red-backed vole, short-tailed shrew, and woodland jumping mouse, the meadow vole is the principal diet of species such as owls, hawks, foxes, and weasels. When the rodent populations are high, so often are the numbers of their predators.

Active throughout the winter, these tiny animals keep mobile in a system of tunnels just beneath the snow surface. Once more than 2.5 cm (1 in) of snow has fallen, meadow vole trails and tunnels in the fields can be easily found and followed.

Laurie and Oakfield Provincial Parks

Length: Laurie Provincial Park –
3 km (2 mi) return
Oakfield Provincial Park – 5 km
(3 mi) return

Hiking Time: 1 hr each

Type of Trail: crushed stone,
natural surface, paved road

Uses: walking, biking*, in-line
skating*, snowshoeing, cross-
country skiing

Facilities: benches, boat launch,
campsites, garbage cans,
outhouses, picnic tables,
unsupervised beach, water

Rating (1-3): 1

Trailhead GPS: Laurie Park Gate –
N 44° 52' 48.9"
W 63° 36' 07.5"
Oakfield Park Gate – N 44° 54'
43.5" W 63° 35' 06.8"

Access Information:

Laurie Provincial Park: From Exit
5 on Highway 102, drive approximately 10 km (6.25 mi) on Highway
2 toward Truro. The park entrance is
on the left. From Exit 6 on Highway
102, drive 8 km (5 mi) on Highway 2
in the direction of Halifax. The park
entrance is on the right

Oakfield Provincial Park: From Exit
5 on Highway 102, drive 12 km (7.5
mi) on Highway 2 toward Truro.
From Exit 6 on Highway 102, drive
5 km (3 mi) on Highway 2 toward
Halifax. Watch for the park sign, and
turn onto a dirt road and drive 1.6
km (1 mi) to the park entrance. If the
gate is open, continue another 1 km
(0.6 mi) to the parking area near the
beach.

Outline: These two small parks, only
a five-minute drive apart, were both
gifts to the province by the Laurie
family, which once owned considerable holdings on and around Grand
Lake. Although the parks are very
busy during the summer, walkers
use them most heavily in autumn
and winter. The routes I have described begin from the park gates,
which are closed after Labour Day.

Laurie Provincial Park: This is both
a picnic and camping park, with 71
campsites that are almost always
filled in the summer. In the fall, the
roads accessing these sites become
quite pleasant shaded walks. In-line

skaters find this a good spot to use roads without fear of traffic. The park may even be more popular in winter than summer because cross-country skiers use it extensively. In fact, it can get so busy that parking becomes crowded around the entrance and spills out onto the highway.

Oakfield Provincial Park: This park is located on the site of a former farm. In addition to the considerable wooded area, there are large open fields available for strolling, and dog owners often come here to let their pets run free. Oakfield is popular in the summer when hundreds flock to its beach and barbecue pits. In the winter, it is popular with cross-country skiers, the fields and paths providing kilometres/miles of possibilities.

Brief Descriptions:

Please note: Laurie Provincial Park will be closed for the 2010 season to accommodate improvements to both the camping and day-use area. A new and improved Laurie Provincial Park will reopen in 2011 offering a central washroom with showers and upgraded campsites.

Laurie Provincial Park: Cross the bridge over the train tracks. When you reach the park administrative centre, take a moment to read the plaque on the monument. The Laurie family donated the land for the park in 1961, and the plaque commemorates their family's long tradition of public service.

Turning right, the road winds down through the picnic area to reach the shores of Grand Lake. Following the road, and keeping the lake on your right, you will reach the boat launch and, beyond that, a parking lot. At the far end of the parking lot is a small signed trail leading through pines. This is the only off-road segment, only a few hundred metres/yards long, and it takes you to a point of land on the shores of Grand Lake that has quite a good view.

From there, continue to follow the road as it heads through the camping area, much of it bordering the lake, until it turns back inland and heads slightly uphill to return to the park office.

* * *

Oakfield Provincial Park: From the gate, walk 1.5 km (0.9 mi) on a gravelled road along the edge of forest and field to the large parking lot at the lake's edge. Beyond a fringe of trees, a grassy hill overlooks the unsupervised beach. An interesting alternative to the road is a walk through the fields on the right. A

Drumlins

The effects of glaciation during the Ice Ages on the Nova Scotia landscape have been dramatic. Ice sheets changed the courses of rivers, scooped out huge valleys, and dumped massive layers of glacial deposits – sometimes as much as 300 m/yd deep – across the province.

In more than 2,300 places in Nova Scotia, deposits of rich glacial till were moulded by the moving ice into oval hills, called drumlins (from the Gaelic, *druim*, meaning mound). Drumlins commonly rise between 15-30 m/yd above the surrounding landscape, and may be as long as one kilometre. They are often found in swarms, which helps distinguish them from other types of hill formations.

Drumlins in Nova Scotia, such as the ones making up much of Oakfield Park, have been extensively farmed and settled because the material making up the hills is often far more fertile than the surrounding lands.

trail created by farm machinery through the grass provides a distinct route.

From the beach, turn left and cross the field to the woods near the out-houses closest to the lake. Cross a bridge over a tiny brook and turn right. Just inside the trees at the edge of the forest, a crushed-stone path traces the shoreline of Grand Lake. For the first 1.5 km (0.9 mi), it works around the tip of a broad point until it reaches an open area where another trail connects. This point was all mature pine until Hurricane Juan flattened nearly every tree. Turn right and continue for a further 250 m/yd, until you reach a small open area at a point of land. Turn away from the lake and start climbing the former estate road up the slopes of the drumlin.

The final 1.5 km (0.9 mi) pass through predominantly mature hemlock and fir, although there are numerous clear patches where hurricane damage obliterated large stands of trees. The trail gradually widens as it climbs the gentle slope of a drumlin and becomes very easy to follow. For almost 1 km (0.6 mi), the path is straight. This beautiful section ends at a junction with a gravelled park road near the main-tenance area. Turn left, and you will find your car about 200 m/yd away, just out of sight on lower ground by the park gate.

Cellphone Coverage: Good throughout.

Cautionary Notes: None.

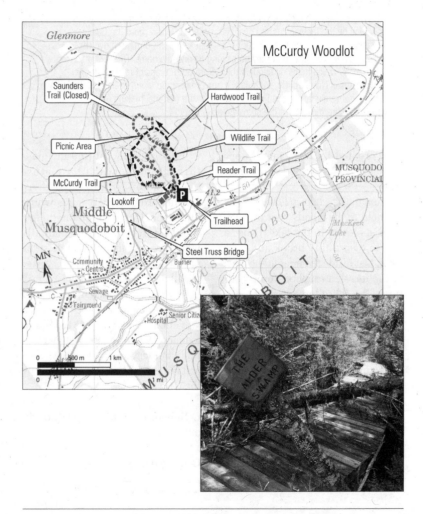

McCurdy Woodlot

Length: 3 km (2 mi) return
Hiking Time: 1 hr
Type of Trail: gravel road, natural
surface, wood chips
Uses: walking, snowshoeing, cross-
country skiing
Facilities: covered tables, garbage
cans, interpretive panels,
outhouses, picnic tables
Rating (1-3): 1
Trailhead GPS: N 45° 03' 17.6"
W 63° 08' 18.0"

Access Information: From Highway
102, take Exit 8 toward Middle Musquodoboit. Follow Highway 277 to
Highway 224 and continue to Middle
Musquodoboit. The McCurdy complex is on the left past the village on
Highway 224 toward Upper Musquodoboit. A large Department of Natural
Resources sign marks the complex. A
dirt road leads uphill 500 m/yd to a
parking lot at the edge of the forest.

Outline: This is a good place to learn
more about Nova Scotia's flora and
fauna. Interpretive sites describe
subjects ranging from common tree
species to bird nesting boxes. The

80 ha (200 ac) woodlot with its trail
system is open to the public year-
round. Brochures can be obtained
from the tourist bureau in Middle
Musquodoboit or (sometimes) at the
trailhead.

Much of the path network is wheelchair accessible with assistance, and
the service road through the middle
of the lot permits shorter walks.
Picnic tables and washrooms at the
far end of the property enable a comfortable break at the halfway mark.
Massive storm damage has closed
portions of the network, particularly
the Saunders Trail.

Brief Description: In the parking lot
sits a large sheltered sign with a map
of the trail system, and copies of
interpretive brochures may also be
available in protected compartments
attached to this display. On your left
are washrooms and a cleared area
with a small pond, lookoff, covered
picnic table, and botanical garden
highlighting the nine main geo-
graphic areas of Nova Scotia.

Follow the Reader Trail, which enters the woods to the right behind the

Water and Filtration

Vigorous walking is a good form of exercise and dehydration can occur quickly. Nothing is more important than having enough drinking water. On hot summer days you can rarely carry enough water; I recommend one litre per person per hour – and one litre of water weighs one kilogram.

You should not plan to drink from any water sources you find while you are hiking. Even lakes and streams that appear pristine may be contaminated with unpleasant bacteria. Portable water filtration units are compact, easy to use, and should ensure that you are able to stay hydrated without running the risk of contracting beaver fever – or worse!

sign. Like all the paths in the woodlot, it contains no difficult grades, and wood chips spread on the treadway cover hidden roots and rocks. Almost immediately, the entrance to the Titus Smith Trail, named after one of Nova Scotia's first environmental scientists, appears on your left. It is an easy 1 km (0.6 mi) walk with 17 stops featuring examples of silvicultural operations, types of vegetation, and enemies of the forest. It works over the forested ridges until ending near an area of picnic tables, shelters, and outhouses.

Many diverse routes are possible, because the woodlot trails are arranged in a maze system. The Wildlife, Fern and Moss, and Saunders (closed in 2010) trails all branch from Titus Smith but eventually reconnect at the picnic ground at the end of the road running through the centre of the woodlot.

From the picnic area, return to the parking lot along the McCurdy Trail. There is another interpretive pathway, this time providing examples of 11 native tree species. The stops will be in reverse order outlined in the brochure with #11, red spruce, your first. Several smaller pathways also branch from McCurdy, including Alex's Path and the Milner Trail. McCurdy emerges from the forest by the Arboretum, about 200 m/yd north of the woodlot entrance sign.

The pattern of interconnecting trails in the woodlot can be confusing, but each loop is so short that you won't remain puzzled for long. You will appreciate the opportunities they provide to vary a hike substantially. The damage caused to the forest by Hurricane Juan and Tropical Storm Noel is apparent everywhere.

Cellphone Coverage: None.

Cautionary Notes: Animals.

Old Annapolis Road

Length: 5 km (3 mi) return
Hiking Time: 2 hrs
Type of Trail: compacted earth, natural surface
Uses: walking, snowshoeing
Facilities: benches, garbage cans, interpretive panels, outhouses
Rating (1-3): 2
Trailhead GPS: N 44° 47' 29" W 63° 36' 38.4"

Access Information: From the Armdale Rotary, follow the St. Margaret's Bay Road, Highway 3, for 4.5 km (2.8 mi). Merge onto Highway 103 West and follow it for 18 km (11.25 mi). Continue past Exit 5. About 3.5 km (2.2 mi) further on Highway 103, as you pass Mill Lake, a dirt road crosses the main highway. Slow carefully and turn right. You immediately see signs for Nova Scotia Power and Bowater Mersey, but the largest sign marks the Old Annapolis Road Hiking Trail; follow the arrow. A gate here, open most of the time, traverses the road. If it is shut, the hiking trail and the woods in this area are off limits. If open, follow the dirt road. At 1.5 km (1 mi), there is a "Y" junction and a sign; turn left. The trailhead is 5 km (3.1 mi) up the dirt road. There is a large parking lot, a sign, and a trailhead pavilion.

Outline: This hiking trail has been in existence for more than 30 years, maintained by Bowater Mersey Paper Company Limited. It is far enough away from the urban centre of the city that it provides relatively undisturbed habitat for wildlife. The hiking trail is open year-round, but the road is not necessarily plowed in winter, or the main gate may be closed due to forest operations in the area.

This is a good walk for schools interested in nature hikes. The main trail is short and quite clear and the parking area big enough for buses. The dirt road to the trailhead is of high quality. It is also a good walk for families with young children. A large display board, located at the entrance to the old road, shows a map of the route, and there are new outhouses in reasonable repair. There is no drinkable water, however.

A segment of this trail follows the path of the former military road constructed between Halifax and Annapolis Royal after the War of 1812. A track was cut through the centre of the province to permit the rapid movements of troops in the event of invasion. Later, discharged soldiers from the conflict were granted land along the road's route.

Brief Description: The trail initially does not follow the old road but enters the forest immediately behind the trailhead pavilion, marked by numerous yellow arrows and hiker symbols. After 200 m/yd, this footpath reconnects with the Old Annapolis Road at a small beach on Rees Lake. Turn right, crossing the bridge over Rees Brook, and continue for barely 150 m/yd before a sign, "Island Lake Loop 1.75 km," directs you left and into the woods onto a winding footpath. Again, yellow metal and wooden arrows sign the route, which is a beautiful path through moss-covered ground.

After travelling briefly through some rough mixed woods, the trail reaches an elevated bridge, high enough to permit canoes to pass beneath, that separates Rees Lake from the much larger Island Lake. Once across, your route alternates between wooded knolls and low-lying marshy areas, traversed by some excellent boardwalks. Once across the second long boardwalk, where there is a bench, your path becomes a rocky trek along the remains of an old wood road. Turn left and follow it uphill, initially through some lovely, new, densely packed softwood growth but then through some extensively storm-damaged areas, until you reach the site of former Logging Camp #2. This grassy field is slowly growing in, but if you look around, you will find some old equipment at the forest edges. There is an interpretive panel and another bench.

Across the clearing, the trail re-enters the woods. Follow the arrows left at the first junction then right at the second. At the next junction, signs indicate that the parking area is 500 m/yd ahead. Instead turn right, following the "Hay Shed Hill Loop 2.2 km" sign. This begins as a delightful old wood road, but within 100 m/yd, you are directed right onto a footpath that wends through the thickly scattered trees. The path drops down a small hill and crosses a wet area; fortunately, there are excellent boardwalk bridges without railings.

There are frequent informal trail junctions, but you should be able to easily stay on the official path.

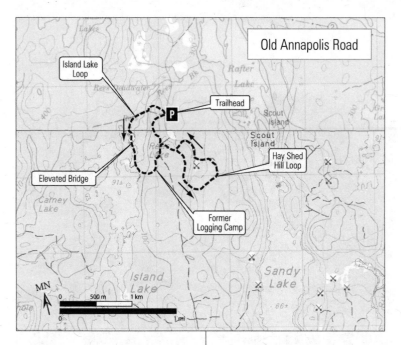

Passing through a magnificent area of red spruce, you will find another interpretive panel situated next to a bench. However, except in the winter, there will probably be too many mosquitoes present to permit a long rest. Continue along the trail, and within a short distance, you will reach and cross the dirt access road about 2.5 km (1.6 mi) from the start.

Watch for a green-and-white hiker symbol on the far side. The path continues through forest, but you should notice an area that has been clear-cut not far to your right. Within a few hundred metres/yards,

you reach another bench and interpretive panel, this one describing commercial forest thinning, situated right on the edge of a clear-cut. Immediately afterwards, the trail turns 90° left and begins its return.

Just before reaching the access road the path curves right, and runs parallel to the automobile route, barely 10-20 m/yd away but sheltered by a thick buffer of vegetation. After several hundred metres/yards, following this overgrown forestry track, the trail swings left and crosses the access road once again. You continue only a short distance before

completing the loop just at the start of the boardwalk over the wet area. Turn right, climb the hill, and return to the signed start of the Hay Shed Hill Loop.

Turn right, where the sign says "Parking Lot 500 m" and follow an attractive, meandering footpath through the spruce trees on the slope just above Rees Lake. There are even a couple of new bridges. The water is sometimes visible, less than 50 m/yd away. Your route does not touch the lake edge again, however, and the path gently descends toward

the Old Annapolis Road. When you reach it, turn right to return to the parking lot.

Cellphone Coverage: Good throughout.

Cautionary Notes: Animals, road crossings.

Polly Cove

Length: 3 km (2 mi) return
Hiking Time: 1 hr
Type of Trail: compacted earth,
  natural surface
Uses: walking, snowshoeing, cross-
  country skiing
Facilities: none
Rating (1-3): 2
Trailhead GPS: N 44° 29' 36.8"
  W 63° 53' 24.5"

Access Information: From the junction of Highway 333 and Highway 3, drive about 33 km (20.5 mi) to West Dover. When you reach the far side of the village, you will pass a ball diamond on the edge of the protected area. Continue toward Peggys Cove for about 800 m/yd. The trail starts to the left at a bend in the road. No signs mark the path, and the parking area is barely large enough for three cars.

Outline: The first part of the walk is an old road that is fairly wide, reasonably dry, and comfortable for almost anybody. Once you leave the road, the footing becomes more challenging and the grades a little steeper, with the vegetation thick and tangled. If you are wearing shorts expect a few scratches.

Most people will not find the paths on the hillsides too difficult, but many walkers turn back at the end of the old road. Good footwear is important if you intend to be scrambling over some of the rougher portions of the walk. Wind conditions will almost certainly be brisk, especially in the fall. Always expect the possibility of wet weather and fog, even when it is sunny in the city.

Some trails need to be walked at a leisurely pace, taking long pauses to adequately absorb the magnificent natural scenery. Polly Cove is one such route. This is also a trail where you should pick a comfortable spot, close your eyes, and listen to the restless, dynamic sounds of the sea.

Brief Description: Follow the old road, which is wide enough for two and reasonably dry, toward the ocean. Trees are few and stunted in these wind-swept barrens, and in the direction of Peggys Cove, the land falls off into a large bog. Your route climbs

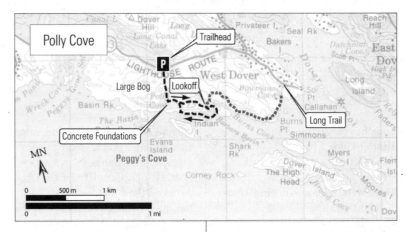

gently for a few hundred metres/ yards, then dips into a depression between several rocks. In this hollow, where the plants are protected from the wind, the vegetation can become quite thick in the summer.

However, the road climbs again, and once you leave the protection of the hills, the trees almost completely disappear. Only the thickly interwoven krummholz of white spruce — trees shaped by the winds and salt spray and stunted by the extreme conditions — surround you now. Within 500 m/yd, you reach the ruins of a fairly large building, only the concrete foundation remaining.

The road ends here, and if you wish to continue, you must follow a narrow footpath to your left. Several footpaths lead through fairly thick brush down the hillside toward the water. Massive granite outcroppings

jut through the thin soil and force the path to detour around them. Initially, Indian Island shelters the trail as it descends into the tiny cove. This only provides temporary protection, however, and soon the trail climbs up the hillside through the brush to the knoll rising above the cove.

Another few hundred metres/ yards and you arrive at your reward, an exposed hilltop with a splendid view of most of the Indian Harbour Barrens. To your left is the village of West Dover and, beyond that, the houses of McGrath Cove and East Dover. Peggys Cove is below and behind you, and on a clear day, you can see the village of Indian Harbour more than 5 km (3 mi) away. Paths lead in all directions, and there is much worth exploring on the coastline below.

🌺 Coastal Barrens

Along the Atlantic coastline, the ocean is the dominant influence on the climate. The landscape along most of the coast is similar to that only a few kilometres inland, but because of the high precipitation, humidity, strong winds, fog, and salt spray, very few plants can survive near the water. The shoreline has had all sediment swept clear by wave action.

Around the exposed headland of the Peggys Cove area, this condition is at its most extreme, with large areas of bleak boulder-strewn hills. In the valleys, few hardy trees other than the dominant white spruce survive, and bogs are common. Rare arctic-alpine flora such as roseroot and fir clubmoss can be found growing in this harsh environment.

This hilltop is a wonderful location to spend a few minutes observing. Then, you can follow one of the many distinct tracks further through the barrens or retrace your route to your car and drive to the restaurant in nearby Peggys Cove for some hot gingerbread and whipped cream!

Cellphone Coverage: Adequate reception on hilltops. No signal at water level.

Cautionary Notes: Rugged terrain, cliffs, high waves during and after storms.

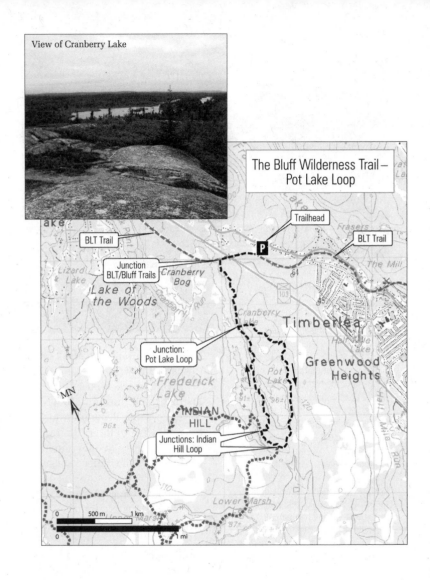

View of Cranberry Lake

The Bluff Wilderness Trail – Pot Lake Loop

Trailhead

BLT Trail

BLT Trail

Junction BLT/Bluff Trails

Junction: Pot Lake Loop

Junctions: Indian Hill Loop

MN

Lizard Lake

Lake of the Woods

Cranberry Bog

Cranberry Run

Cranberry Lake

Timberlea

Half Mile Lake

Greenwood Heights

Frederick Lake

INDIAN HILL

Lower Marsh

Half Mile Run

Frasers

The Mill

0   500 m   1 km

0   1 mi

The Bluff Wilderness Trail – Pot Lake Loop

Length: 10 km (6.25 mi) return
Hiking Time: 3-4 hrs
Type of Trail: crushed stone, natural surface, rocks
Uses: walking, biking*, ATV*, snowshoeing, cross-country skiing*, snowmobiling*
Facilities: bike racks, garbage cans
Rating (1-3): 3
Trailhead GPS: N 44° 39' 55.4" W 63° 45' 47.1"

Access Information: From the Armdale Rotary, follow the St. Margaret's Bay Road, Highway 3, for 4.5 km (2.8 mi). Merge onto Highway 103 West and follow it for 11 km (6.9 mi) to Exit 4. Turn right onto Highway 3 and continue for 2 km (1.25 mi). The trailhead is on the right, at 2890 Highway 3.

The closest Metro Transit stop is route 21 at Forestglen Drive with the intersection of Fraser Road, a 1.5 km (0.9 mi) walk to the trailhead along the Beechville Lakeside Timberlea (BLT) abandoned rail line, part of the Trans Canada Trail.

Outline: Few expect to find such a large, isolated area so close to downtown Halifax, but the challenging terrain, mostly barrens supporting dense brush unsuitable for either harvesting wood or for agriculture, has meant that few other than hunters ever venture here. Small populations of bear and even the rare mainland moose reside here, within 30 km (19 mi) of downtown Halifax.

Threatened by the rapid growth of the urban area, the crown lands in this area, known as the Chebucto, or Five Bridge Lakes, became the focus of the preservation efforts of a number of groups. One of these, the Woodens River Watershed Environmental Organization, built an extensive wilderness hiking trail in an effort to allow the community to become aware of the natural beauty of the area. On October 19, 2009, the provincial environment minister announced the government's intention to designate 8,266 ha (20,425 ac) of crown lands in the Five Bridge Lakes area of Halifax

Regional Municipality (HRM) as a wilderness area.

The Bluff Wilderness Hiking Trail system is made up of four stacked loops of more than 30 km (18.75 mi). In this book, I have profiled only the first of these, the Pot Lake Loop.

Brief Description: Turn right when you exit the parking lot. For the first 550 m/yd, you walk along the wide, crushed-stone-surfaced multi-use BLT Trail. Cyclists and ATV users are common, so keep to the right and do not block the trail when part of a group. You will notice a speed limit of 20 kph (12.5 mph) for bikes and ATVs as well as the BLT's 7 km (4.2 mi) marker. At 400 m/yd, the trail crosses beneath Highway 103 through two impressively massive culverts. Young, healthy-looking larch line much of this section.

About 50 m/yd beyond the culverts is the official entrance to The Bluff Wilderness Trail system to your left. A bike rack and garbage can sit next to a large sign, which includes a map. The sign warns that this is an unsupervised route suitable for experienced hikers. Only walking is permitted on the Pot Lake Loop.

The first 1 km (0.6 mi) provides an indication of the challenges you will encounter. A narrow footpath, the trail meanders through dense vegetation and crosses several boardwalks over substantial wet areas, Cranberry Lake to your right. Initially quite distinct, once across the second, long boardwalk, just past the bear and moose warning sign, the path becomes significantly less clear. Watch closely for the yellow metal route markers, and for painted arrows — regrettably coloured black — on the rocks where the route crosses extensive areas of barrens.

Climbing at first, which provides excellent views of Cranberry Lake, the trail drops swiftly to water level at 1 km (0.6 mi), where you find the junction with the Pot Lake Loop. This is well marked, with a map and a printed sign "Pot Lake Loop 2-3 hrs·return." Turn left, away from the lake.

Immediately you begin a rugged, rocky, steep climb over moss-covered

Bunchberry

Barrens like the land around Peggys Cove are an ideal habitat for a common Nova Scotia herb, the bunchberry. Bunchberries also thrive in heath, the edge of thickets, and bogs, and often grow in thick carpets beneath softwoods. In the fall, when the bright red berries are clustered together in the centre of each plant, it is easy to understand how these plants received their name. In June, small, greenish-white flowers adorn the plants, providing a welcome splash of colour to the harsh landscape.

The berries are edible, although the hard seed at the centre makes them difficult for humans to eat. Some bird species enjoy them much more.

granite and greywacke, hemmed by thick white spruce. Although brief, this section is challenging. After perhaps 400 m/yd, you emerge onto a huge flat rock, where the route is marked by small piles of stones and painted black arrows. The path continues to wander between thick forest and open rock, continuously climbing and descending and working its way around the many wet areas. Massive boulders loom through the trees to your left, and there are sections where the woods seem gloomy and confining.

You walk almost 2 km (1.25 mi) from the junction before you actually reach the shore of Pot Lake, and the trail keeps you beside it only briefly — reaching water level only once — before turning away into the forest to skirt another large swampy area at the lake's south end. Within seconds, you are immersed in thick vegetation, the lake hidden from view. Your twisting path eventually brings you out into areas of open rocks, and it is on one of these that you find the junction, marked by a map, with the Indian Hill Loop. You have walked 5 km (3.1 mi).

Turn right, where after 700 m/yd of similar terrain, which provides views of Pot Lake to your right and barrens to your left, you reach the second junction with the Indian Hill Loop, also marked with a map. This is a wonderful location, with the best views yet. Cranberry Lake is directly ahead, and with binoculars, you can even see traffic on Highway 103. Small Pot Lake is to your right.

Blisters

Even the most careful hiker will get blisters. Left untreated, they can turn the shortest walk into a painful nightmare. Treat a blister like an open wound: clean it with soap and water and dress it with Second Skin. If your feet are dirty or sweaty, clean them with an alcohol-saturated wipe to help adhesive tape adhere.

Vaseline

Prone to blisters? My grandfather taught me to thickly smear my feet with Vaseline, especially between my toes. He told me that if I did so, I would never get a blister, no matter how far I walked. And as long as I've used Vaseline, I never have, even when I ran marathons. Thanks Grandad!

Turn right, following the yellow marked path. Surprisingly, what follows is some of this route's most difficult trekking, as you worm through narrow defiles between rocky ridges and work your way around the many scattered boulders, glacial erratics. The path drops onto a slender corridor of land separating Cranberry and Pot lakes. Some of the trail lies beneath pine, and the tread here is carpeted in fallen needles.

But much of this area is wet, and just before you cross the little stream between the two lakes — without benefit of a bridge — you encounter a signed canoe portage route.

Once across the creek, you climb out of the wet zone and its canopy of softwoods into an area of hardwoods. The trail parallels Cranberry Lake, working its way up the slope and into an area of huge glacial boulders. This is difficult walking, and when you descend back to the water level, it is sudden and steep, back into a dense stand of young white spruce. There is a short boardwalk before you arrive back at the Pot Lake Loop Junction, having walked 8.5 km (5.3 mi).

Continue straight, retracing your route back to the BLT Trail and the trailhead.

Cellphone Coverage: Good throughout.

Cautionary Notes: Animals, hunting in season, isolated, rugged terrain.

Acknowledgements

Acknowledgements are enjoyable to write in any book. After all, how often does a person get to publicly thank the people who have provided help and guidance? And no less importantly, without the excellent assistance of so many people, *Trails of Halifax Regional Municipality, 2nd Edition*, would be far less accurate than it is.

Regrettably, so many people provided me with information and feedback that it would be impossible to name them all without missing a good many of them. Several trail managers reviewed my draft text for their systems and suggested improvements. Staff from the Department of Natural Resources examined my material in order to ensure accuracy and answered numerous questions. Members of a number of the provincial trail associations offered suggestions and encouragement at all stages of this project.

As always, a few individuals merit special mention. Jim Vance, my successor as Executive Director of the Nova Scotia Trail Federation and a tireless advocate of the Inter-national Appalachian Trail, hiked with me when I was checking some of the routes. Don Ambler, a Trail Specialist with the Halifax Regional Municipality, spent a considerable period of time escorting me to new trails developed in the past several years and was always prompt in responding to my requests for information, as were his co-workers, Jessie Debaie, Dawn Neil, and Paul Euloth. My parents, John and Joan Haynes, hosted me for an entire month while I re-walked every route. (I think putting up with me as a guest for 30 days deserves special "bonus" thanks!) My wife, Elina, accepted my long absence from our home with understanding, and her daily phone calls were more valuable to me than I can express.

Mostly, however, I wish to thank the trail development community in Nova Scotia for the tremendous progress that they have made in the past decade. Those outside that community cannot begin to understand how much effort has gone into building, improving, and maintaining the impressive network

of managed walking and biking trails that can be found within the boundaries of the Halifax Regional Municipality. It is a very different system than existed when the first edition of *Trails of Halifax Regional Municipality* was published in 1999, and there is every indication that it is going to continue to improve even more over the next decade.

A book about hiking could not be possible if no trails existed. Thanks to the members of the Nova Scotia Trails Federation and its member clubs of volunteers, including Hike Nova Scotia, who supplied their vision and energy. Thanks to the Nova Scotia Department of Health Promotion and Protection, Nova Scotia Environment, and the Department of Natural Resources for nurturing and supporting these volunteers and for their efforts to promote trail development and use. Thanks to the Halifax Regional Municipality for becoming one of Canada's leaders in trails.

There are so many people I could have mentioned. I hope that those whom I have missed will forgive me, and know that I recognize and value their contribution, even if that gratitude is not explicitly stated

Michael Haynes
March 31, 2010

Updates from the First Edition

A number of trails profiled in the first edition of *Trails of Halifax Regional Municipality* were not included in this volume and some others were added. For those who own the first edition, this is an update on the status of trails that have been dropped, those that have significantly changed, and new additions.

Halifax–Dartmouth:

Cole Harbour Heritage Park: separated into two route descriptions — Cole Harbour Heritage Park (route changed) and Salt Marsh Trail.

Dartmouth Multi-use Trail: routes changed to Sullivans Pond and Lake Micmac sections.

Hemlock Ravine Park: route changed.

Mainland North Linear Parkway: route changed.

Vivien's Way: new trail.

Eastern Shore:

Crowbar Lake Trail: new trail.

Gibraltar Rock Loop: new trail.

McCormack's Beach: dropped from this edition.

Rainbow Haven: dropped from this edition.

Salt Marsh Trail: formerly part of Cole Harbour Heritage Park; route changed.

Shearwater Flyer: new trail.

Central–South Shore:

Bedford Sackville Connector Greenway: route changed.

First and Second Lake Trails: new trails.

McCurdy Woodlot: route changed.

Old Annapolis Valley Road: route changed.

The Bluff Wilderness Trail–Pot Lake Loop: new trail.

Web Pages

The URLs listed below were current as of April 2010. Regrettably, organizations seem to regularly change their Web addresses, so if you find a listed link does not work, I recommend that you copy the site's name and paste it into your preferred Internet Search Engine. This should direct you to the new link.

Updated links will be posted on the *Trails of the Halifax Regional Municipality, 2nd Edition* blog: http://hikinghrm.blog spot.com/

On-line full-colour maps of each of the routes profiled in *Trails of Halifax Regional Municipality, 2nd Edition*, are available for purchase at MapSherpa: www.mapsherpa.com

A. Outdoor Associations:

Beechville Lakeside Timberlea Rails to Trails Association: www.blttrails.ca

Bicycle Nova Scotia: www.bicycle.ns.ca

Canadian Volkssport Federation: www.walks.ca

Chebucto Hiking Club: http://chc.chebucto.org/

Climb Nova Scotia: www.climbnova scotia.ca

Dartmouth Volksmarch Club: www.dartmouthvolksmarchclub.com

Explore Nova Scotia: www.explore novascotia.com

Friends of McNabs Island Society: www.chebucto.ns.ca/environment/FOMIS

Halifax Field Naturalists: http://halifax fieldnaturalists.ca/hfnWP/

Halifax Outdoor Adventurers: www.meetup.com/Halifax-Outdoors

Hike Nova Scotia: www.hikenovascotia.ca

Nova Scotia Bird Society: www.chebucto.ns.ca/Recreation/NS-BirdSoc/

Nova Scotia Trails Federation: www.novascotiatrails.com

Orienteering Association of Nova Scotia: http://orienteeringns.ca

Shubenacadie Canal Commission: http://shubie.chebucto.org

Trail Information Project: www.trails.gov.ns.ca

Trans Canada Trail: www.tctrail.ca

Velo Halifax Bicycle Club: www.velo halifax.ca/

B. Park/Trail Websites:

BLT Trail: www.halifax.ca/rec/documents/BLT_000.pdf

Cole Harbour Heritage Park: http://chpta.blogspot.com/2008/06/halifax-county-poors-farm-bissett-road.html

Cole Harbour Parks and Trails Association: http://chpta.blogspot.com

Halifax Regional Municipality — Trails: www.halifax.ca/rec/TrailsHrm.html

Musquodoboit Trailway Association: www.mta-ns.ca

St. Margaret's Bay Rails to Trails: www.

halifax.ca/rec/documents/SMBRails
ToTrails.pdf

Taylor Head Provincial Park: http://parks.
gov.ns.ca/brochures/TaylorHeadTrail.
pdf

The Bluff Wilderness Hiking Trail: www.
wrweo.ca/BluffTrail

York Redoubt National Historic Site:
www.pc.gc.ca/lhn-nhs/ns/york/index.
aspx

C. Animals:

Bear Brochure, Parks Canada: www.pc.
gc.ca/pn-np/inc/PM-MP/visit/visit
12a_e.pdf

Birds of Nova Scotia: http://museum.gov.
ns.ca/mnh/nature/nsbirds/bons.htm

Bobcat Information: www.gov.ns.ca/natr/
wildlife/CONSERVA/bobcat.asp

Cougar Information: www.hww.ca/hww2.
asp?id=87

Coyote Information: www.gov.ns.ca/natr/
wildlife/nuisance/coyotes-faq.asp

Moose Information: www.hww.ca/hww2.
asp?id=93

D. General Interest:

Atlantic Canada Geocaching Association:
http://www.atlanticgeocaching.com

Explore Nova Scotia: www.explorenova
scotia.com

Halifax Regional Municipality — Walking:
www.halifax.ca/rec/Walking.html

Heart & Stroke Walkabout: www.walk
aboutns.ca

Keep It Wild Brochure: www.gov.ns.ca/
nse/protectedareas/docs/KeepItWild_
recreation.pdf

Leave No Trace Canada: www.leaveno
trace.ca

Natural History of Nova Scotia: http://
museum.gov.ns.ca/mnh/nature/nhns

Nova Scotia Department of Natural
Resources: www.gov.ns.ca/natr

Nova Scotia Museum of Natural History:
http://museum.gov.ns.ca/mnh

Nova Scotia Museum, Natural History
Publications: http://museum.gov.ns.
ca/en/home/educationalresources/
publications/naturalhistory.aspx

Nova Scotia Provincial Park Events:
www.novascotiaparks.ca/misc/park_
events.asp

Parks Canada: www.pc.gc.ca

Province of Nova Scotia Wilderness
Protected Areas: www.gov.ns.ca/nse/
protectedareas/wildernessareas.asp

The Big Wild: www.thebigwild.org

Tick Information, Public Health Agency
of Canada: www.phac-aspc.gc.ca/id-
mi/tickinfo-eng.php#es

Trees of Nova Scotia: http://www.gov.
ns.ca/natr/forestry/treeid/

E. Weather

Video — Storm Surge, Peggys Cove,
Hurricane Bill: www.youtube.com/
watch?v=TQzdUW7xqmI

Weather Network: www.theweather
network.com/weather/cans0057

F. Cellphone Coverage

Bell: www.bell.ca/support/PrsCSrvWls_
Cvg_Travel.page

Rogers: http://your.rogers.com/business/
custservice/coverage/info.asp#Page_2

Telus: www.telusmobility.com/en/ON/
Coverageandtravelling/canadavoice
maps.shtml

G. Transit

Metro Transit: www.halifax.ca/metro
transit

H. Dog Regulations:

Halifax Regional Municipality: www.halifax.ca/animalcontrol/Dogs.html

Off Leash Areas Information: http://www.halifax.ca/realpropertyplanning/OLPS/olps_maps.html

Pet Friendly Travel: www.petfriendlytravel.com/dog_parks_canada

Point Pleasant Park: www.pointpleasantpark.ca/en/home/thingstoknow/dogs/default.aspx

I. Hurricane Juan:

Point Pleasant Park Photo Gallery: www.halifax.ca/emo/juan/juanslidesPP.html

Point Pleasant Park International Design Competition: www.pointpleasantpark.ca/site-ppp/competitionwebsite/ppp.isl.ca/inside39ca.html?cmPageID=83

Index

Please note: All quick tips are indicated with subject and page numbers in bold.
All sidebar subjects are indicated with page numbers in italics.

A

abandoned railroads 84
Abraham Lake 8, 69-70
Abraham Lake Nature Reserve 15, 23, 68-70
Admiral Lake 72
Admiral Lake Lookoff 72
Admiral Lake Loop 12, 15, 71-74, 97
Aerotech Business Park 129
alder 110, 115, *130*
Alex's Path 142
Amherst 97
Annapolis Royal 144
Anne Dodge Trail 116
Annie Blois Trail 114, 116
Arboretum 142
aspen 24
Atlantic Interior 41
Atlantic Ocean 72, 103
Atlantic Ocean Lookoff 73
Atlantic View Trail 88-89

B

backpack 13
bandana 105
Banook Canoe Club 32
barrier beaches 90
Bay of Fundy 26, 59
Bayer Lake 71-72
Bayers Islands 91-93
Bayers Point 93
beach grass, American 118
Beach Sand Sculpture Contest 75
Beach Walk Trail 104
bears 11, 13

Beaver House Trail, 115
Beaverdam Brook 40-41
beavers 113, 115, 116, 130
Bedford 13, 109
Bedford Basin 18, 34
Bedford Place Mall 109-110
Bedford Sackville Connector Greenway 16, 108-111
Beechville Lakeside Timberlea Trail 151-154
Big Paul's Loop 116
binoculars 13, 71
birch 70, 72, 115, 130
   white 24
Bissett Lake Bridge 99, 101
Bissett Road Farm 29
Black Rock Beach 47, 48
blackflies 114
blisters 154
BLT Trail. *See* Beechville Lakeside Timberlea Trail
blueberries 120
Bluff Wilderness Trail 7, 150-154, 159
Bluff Wilderness Trail–Pot Lake Loop 12, 16, 127, 150-154
Bobs Bluff 16, 106
Bobs Bluff Beach 103, 106
Bowater Mersey Paper Company Limited 143
Brook Trail 28
bug repellent 13
Bull Beach 16, 103, 106
Bull Beach Trail 104
bunchberry 153

Burnt Island 77
Burnt Point 76, 77

C

call of nature 111
Cambridge Battery 49
camera 13, 71, **95**
Canadian Forces Naval Construction
Troop (Atlantic) 96
Canadian Naval Engineering School
Damage Control School 65
Canadian Pacific Railway 57
Canadian Volkssport Federation 158
Cape Breton Highlands 7
Cape Chignecto Provincial Park 7
Cave, The 73
cellphone 11, 45, **95**
Centennial Pond 49
Central – South Shore 121, 124-127
Chain Lakes 39
Charles L. MacDonald Sports Park 16,
113-116, 124
Chebucto 151
Citadel 64
Clam Bay 76, 90
Clam Harbour 75, 77
Clam Harbour Beach Provincial Park 15,
67, 75, 77
Climb Nova Scotia 158
coastal barrens 149
Cole Harbour 26, 87
Cole Harbour Heritage Park 15, 25-29
Cole Harbour/Lawrencetown Coastal
Heritage Park System 88
Cole Harbour Parks and Trails
Association 27, 159
Cole Harbour Salt Marsh 26-27, 96
compass 12, **104**
Conrad Beach 87, 89
Conrad Brothers 96
Cooks Brook 60
Coote Cove 117-120
Costley Farm Trail 28
cougars 13

County of Halifax 29
coyotes 11, *53*
Cranberry Lake 150-154
Cranberry Pond 39-40
Crowbar Lake 78-81
Crowbar Lake Trail 12, 16, 79
Crystal Crescent Beach 117
Crystal Crescent Beach Provincial Park
16, 117-121

D

Dartmouth 8, 13, 25, 31, 59, 71, 75, 83,
91
Dartmouth Air Station Flyers 98
Dartmouth Multi-use Trail 15, 30-33,
51-52, 97
Dartmouth Volksmarch Club 158
De Said Lake Bridge 99
Debaie, Jessie 155
deer 37
white-tailed 36
Department of National Defence 109
Firing Range 110-111
Dingle Cove 57
Dingle Tower 55-57
Discover McNabs Island 63
Dollar Lake 130-131
Dollar Lake Brook 130
Dollar Lake Provincial Park 16, 128-131
drumlins 24, *139*
ducks 31, 50, 55, 56, 91, 95, 104
black 36
mallard 36
dunes 118

E

eagle, bald 74
East Dover 148
East Lawrencetown 89
East Petpeswick 91
Eastern Passage 63, 100
Eastern Shore 23, 83, 122, 123, 129
East Section 16, 99
eel 109

elevated bridge 125
Elhorn, Patrick 84
Environment Canada 33, 48
etiquette 33
Euloth, Paul 155
Eunice Lake 72

F
Fairbanks Centre 33, 50, 53
Fairview Cove 34
Fern Trail 142
ferns 70
field guides 13
filtration 142
fir 139
Fire Command Post 65
first-aid kit 13
First and Second Lake Trails 16, 133-135
First Lake 16, 133
First Lake Trail 132-133
Five Bridge Lakes 151
flashlight 65
Fleming, Sir Sandford 57
Flying Point 93, 96
food 12
footwear 12, 65
Fort Clarence 64
Fort Ives 64
Fort Needham 64
fox 136
  red 88
Friends of McNabs Island Society, The
  63, 158
Frog Pond 55-56
frogs 113
Front Country Paths 27
Fultz House Museum 111

G
GPS 104
garbage bag 13, **134**
gaspereau 109
Gate House, Point Pleasant Park 49
geese 31, 91, 95

Geizer Hill 44
Georges Island 64
Gibraltar Loop Trail 83
Gibraltar Rock 83-84
Gibraltar Rock Loop 16, 82-85
Glasgow Island 96-97
Goffs 129
Goodwood 39, 40
Governor Lake 69
Governor's Loop 36-37
GPS. *See* Global Positioning System
Grahams Grove Park 32
Grand Lake 137-139
Granite Lake 81
Granite Ridge 83
Grassy Brook 32
Grosvenor/Wentworth Park School 34,
  37
gulls 31

H
Halifax fortifications 64
Halifax Harbour 47, 48, 59, 60, 63, 89,
  117
Halifax Outdoor Adventurers 158
Halifax West High School 44
Hangman's Beach, York Redoubt 63
Harbour Point 77
hare
  snowshoe 53, 130
Harrietsfield 39
hat 13
hawks 136
Hay Shed Hill Loop 144, 146
Headland Trail 104
Heart and Stroke Foundation 44
  Walkabout 159
hemlock 36, 37, 69, 70, 79, 84, 116, 139
  eastern 68, *36*
Hemlock Ravine 20, 34, 36, 38
Hemlock Ravine Park 15, 34-38
Heritage Road 29
Heritage Trail 27-29

herons 95-96
  blue 26
Herring Cove 21
HMCS *Bonaventure* 48
hunting season 14, **152**
Hurricane Juan 28, 36-37, 41, 47, *48*, 80, 85, 96, 129, 139, 142
hypothermia 88

I

Indian Harbour 148
Indian Harbour Barrens 148
Indian Hill Loop 153
Indian Island 148
Intercolonial Railway 57
Island Lake 144
Island Lake Loop 144

J

jacket, rain 12
jeans, blue 114
Jerry Lonecloud Trail 28
Jersey Jack Trail 28
Jessie's Diner 72
Julie's Pond 18, 36
juniper 105

K

Karen Furneaux Trail 116
Keep It Wild Brochure 159
Kejimkujik National Park 7
Kelly Junction 85
Kent, Prince Edward, Duke of 18
kingfisher 61
knife 12
krummholz 105, *123*

L

Labrador 26
lady's slipper 72
Lake Banook 31-33
Lake Charles 33, 50, 52, 59-61
Lake Charlotte 75
Lake Echo 87

Lake Micmac 15, 31-32, 50, 53, 157
Lake Thomas 113-114
larch 105, 152
Laurie family 137-138
Laurie Provincial Park 16, 136-139
Lawlor Island 63, 100
Lawrencetown Beach 87, 89, 90
Lawrencetown Beach Provincial Park 16, 86, 87, 88, 89
Lawrencetown Beach Trail 97
Lawrencetown Bridge 89
Lawrencetown Head 88-89
Lawrencetown Lake 87-89
Lawrencetown Provincial Beach 118
Lawrencetown River 89
layering 56
Leave No Trace 44, 159
lichen 72, 105
Liscomb Game Sanctuary 69
Little Sackville River 111
Logging Camp #2 144
Long Island 76
Long Lake 39, 40, 41, 53
Long Lake Provincial Park 15, 38-41
Long Trail 69-70
loons 70
Lower Sackville 13, 113, 133-134
Lyme disease 110

M

MacDonald's Tea Room and Cake Shop 89
Mackerel Cove 120
Mackerel Cove Beach 120
Mad Rock 117
Mainland North Common 44
Mainland North Linear Parkway 15, 42-45
map 12, 104
maple 70
marshes, tidal 26
Martello Tower National Historic Site 49
Martinique Beach 90-93

Martinique Beach Game Sanctuary 91
Martinique Beach Provincial Park 16, 90-93, 122, 123
matches 12
Mayflower 116
McCurdy Trail 142
McCurdy Woodlot 16, 140-142
McGrath Cove 148
McNabs Island 62-64
McNabs Island Lighthouse 63
Metro Transit 11, 160
mice, deer 136
   woodland jumping 136
Micmac Aquatic Club 32
Micmac Campsite 60
MicMac Mall 53
Middle Musquodoboit 141
Middle Point 93
Mill Lake 143
Milner Trail 142
moose 13, 130
Morris Lake Bridge 99
moss 72
   fir club 149
Moss Trail 142
Mushaboom Harbour 104
Musquodoboit Harbour 71, 83, 91, 93, 129
Musquodoboit Rail Trail 98
Musquodoboit River 71, 74, 81, 83
Musquodoboit River Valley 72
Musquodoboit Valley 82, 131

N
National Topographic System of Canada 12
Natural History of Nova Scotia 159
Nature Conservancy of Canada 14, 69
New Glasgow 69
Newcombe's Graveyard 104
Nine Mile River 17
North Granite Ridge Trail 85
North Sydney 97
Northumberland Strait 93

Northwest Arm 43, 49, 56-57
Nova Scotia Department of Natural Resources 14, 39, 141
Nova Scotia Power 143
Nova Scotia Trails Federation 156
Nude Beach 120

O
oak 116
Oakfield Provincial Park 16, 107, 136-139
Off Leash Areas Information 160
Old Annapolis Road 125, 143-146
Old Annapolis Road Hiking Trail 143
Old Annapolis Valley Road 16
Old Beaver House Trail 116
Old Stagecoach Trail 116, 124
Olivers Cove 131
owls 136

P
Paddlers Cove 32
Panorama Trail 28
paper, writing 13
Park West School 45
Parks Canada 13, 159, 160
Peggys Cove 147-149, 153
pen 13
Penhorn Mall 27, 95
Pennant Point 118, 120-121
Peter McNab Kuhn Conservation Area 28, 96
Peters Lake 39
Petpeswick Inlet 73
pigeons 31
pine 33, 47, 48, 79, 139, 154
   Jack 24, 56, 84
   white 68
Pine Corner 60
pitcher plant 127
plover, piping 93
Point Pleasant Battery 49
Point Pleasant Park 15, 36, 46-49
poison ivy 13, **35**, 100

Polly Cove 16, 126, 147-149
Poor's Farm 27
Poor's Farm Reservoir 28
Poor's Farm Road 28-29
poplar 115
porcupine 135
Porters Lake 81
Portobello Inclined Plane 59
Pot Lake 153-154
Pot Lake Loop 152-154
Prince's Lodge 18
Prince's Park, The 18
Psyche Cove 104
Purcell's Cove Ferry 49

Q
Quarry Pond 49
Queen Anne's lace 110

R
Rail Trail 85
railroads 84
Rainbow Haven 96
Range Park 110
Ravine Trail 37
Reader Trail 141
Rees Brook 144
Rees Lake 144, 146
Rockingham Loop 37
Rockingham Ridge Park 45
Rogers 160
Rolling Stone Lookoff 73
Rosemary's Way 96
roseroot 149
roses, wild 110
Royal Colonial Institute of London 57
Run Brook, The 28

S
Sack-A-Wa Canoe Club 133-134
Sackville Lakes District 133
Sackville River 109-111
Sailors' Memorial Way 48-49
St. Laurent, Julie 18

St. Laurent Trail 37
St. Margaret's Bay Rails to Trails 98
salamanders 113
Sally port 65, 66
salmon, Atlantic 109
Salt Marsh Trail 16, 27-29, 84, 88, 94-99
Sambro 117
Sambro Harbour 117, 119
Sambro Island 117
Saunders Trail 141-142
School Trail 37
Scott Maritimes Ltd. 68
sea trout 109
seals 106
Second Lake 16, 133-135
Second Lake Regional Park Association
   133
Second Lake Trail 132
Senobe Aquatic Canoe Club 32
Shag Rock 117
Shakespeare-By-The-Sea 48
Shearwater 63
Shearwater Air Base 98-100
Shearwater Flyer Trail 16, 27, 84, 88,
   97-101
Shearwater Flyers 98
Sheet Harbour 69, 103
Shirley-Anne Trail 113-114
shoelaces 85
shorebirds 95
Short Trail 69-70
shrews 136
Shubenacadie Canal 32, 33, 50, 52,
   59-60
Shubenacadie Canal Commission 50
Shubenacadie Canal Trail 59, 61
Shubie Municipal Campground 51-52
Shubie Park 32, 50, 59
Shubie Park–Canal 15, 20, 50-53
Sir Sandford Fleming Park 15, 54-57
Sisters, The 117
Skull Rock 74
snakes 14
socks 52

sparrow, song 103
Special Places Protection Act 69
Spriggs Brook 80-81
Spriggs Brook Bridge 80-81
spruce 36, 70, 73, 81, 84, 105
　black 24
　red 68, 69, 70, 142, 145
　white 89, 93, 123, 148, 149, 152, 154
Spruce Hill Lake 39
Spry Bay 16, 103, 105
Spry Bay Trail 104
Spryfield 41
Srivastava, Vivien 61
Stinky Brook 28-29
Stoddard family 75
Stoney Beach 89
Sullivans Pond 31-32, 157
sunscreen 13
sweater 12

T
Taylor Head Provincial Park 16, 102-106
Taylors Head Bay 106
Telus 160
Terence Bay Candidate Protected Area
　39
ticks 14, *110*, 160
　American dog 14
tidal marshes 26
Titus Smith Trail 142
toilet paper 13
Trail Information Project 158
Trans Canada Trail 7, 32, 71, 72, 83, 88,
　96, *97*, 152
Trees of Nova Scotia 160
Trinity Anglican Church 43, 44
Tropical Storm Noël 142
True North Diner 109
Truro 97, 129, 137
turtles 113

U
Upper Musquodoboit 141

V
Vance, Jim 155
vaseline 154
Veterans Memorial 31
virgin's bower 110
Vivien's Way 15, 22, 58-61
voles
　meadow *136*
　red-backed 136

W
WAAA. *See* Waverly Amateur Athletic
　Association
War of 1812 144
warblers 110
water 12, 71, **142**
Water Commission 39
Waverley 113, 133
Waverley Amateur Athletic Association
　113
Waverley–Salmon River Long Lake
　Wilderness Protected Area 7, 79
weasels 136
weather 14
Weather Network 160
Wentworth, Lieutenant-Governor John
　18
Wentworth Loop 37
West Dover 147-148
West Lake Loop 81
West Section 16, 99
Whale Point 92
whistle 12, **95**
White Lake Protected Area 74
Whites Lake Wilderness Ridge Trail 72
Whites Lake Wilderness Protected Area
　7, 83
Wilderness Protected Areas 7, *81*, 160
Wilderness Trail 85
Wildlife Trail 142
willow 115
Witherod Lake 39
Woodens River Watershed
　Environmental Organization 151

World Meteorological Organization 33, 48
World War I 49
World War II 49, 62, 64, 65, 84

Y
York Redoubt 62-64
York Redoubt National Historic Site 15, 21, 62-66, 159
York Shore Battery 65